VATICAN COUNCIL II
THE NEW DIRECTION

RELIGIOUS PERSPECTIVES
Planned and Edited by
RUTH NANDA ANSHEN

RELIGIOUS PERSPECTIVES · VOLUME NINETEEN

VATICAN COUNCIL II THE NEW DIRECTION

by Oscar Cullmann

Essays
Selected and Arranged by
James D. Hester

HARPER & ROW, PUBLISHERS

New York, Evanston, and London

FIRST EDITION

B-S

LIBRARY OF CONGRESS CATALOG CARD NUMBER: 68-11981

CONTENTS

RELIGIOUS PERSPECTIVES

VOLUMES ALREADY PUBLISHED

7

RELIGIOUS PERSPECTIVES

Its Meaning and Purpose

RELIGIOUS PERSPECTIVES represents a quest for the rediscovery of man. It constitutes an effort to define man's search for the essence of being in order that he may have a knowledge of goals. It is an endeavor to show that there is no possibility of achieving an understanding of man's total nature on the basis of phenomena known by the analytical method alone. It hopes to point to the false antinomy between revelation and reason, faith and knowledge, grace and nature, courage and anxiety. Mathematics, physics, philosophy, biology, and religion, in spite of their almost complete independence, have begun to sense their interrelatedness and to become aware of that mode of cognition which teaches that "the light is not without but within me, and I myself am the light."

Modern man is threatened by a world created by himself. He is faced with the conversion of mind to naturalism, a dogmatic secularism and an opposition to a belief in the transcendent. He begins to see, however, that the universe is given not as one existing and one perceived but as the unity of subject and object; that the barrier between them cannot be said to have been dissolved as the result of recent experience in the physical sciences, since this barrier has never existed. Confronted with the question of meaning, he is summoned to rediscover and scrutinize the immutable and the permanent which constitute the dynamic, unifying aspect of life as well as the principle of differentiation; to reconcile identity and diversity, immutability and unrest. He begins to recognize that just as every person descends by his particular path, so he is able to ascend, and this ascent aims at a return to the source of creation, an inward home from which he has become estranged.

It is the hope of RELIGIOUS PERSPECTIVES that the rediscovery of man will point the way to the rediscovery of God. To this end a

9

rediscovery of first principles should constitute part of the quest. These principles, not to be superseded by new discoveries, are not those of historical worlds that come to be and perish. They are to be sought in the heart and spirit of man, and no interpretation of a merely historical or scientific universe can guide the search. RELIGIOUS PERSPECTIVES attempts not only to ask dispassionately what the nature of God is, but also to restore to human life at least the hypothesis of God and the symbols that relate to him. It endeavors to show that man is faced with the metaphysical question of the truth of religion while he encounters the empirical question of its effects on the life of humanity and its meaning for society. Religion is here distinguished from theology and its doctrinal forms and is intended to denote the feelings, aspirations, and acts of men, as they relate to total reality. For we are all in search of reality, of a reality which is there whether we know it or not; and the search is of our own making but reality is not.

RELIGIOUS PERSPECTIVES is nourished by the spiritual and intellectual energy of world thought, by those religious and ethical leaders who are not merely spectators but scholars deeply involved in the critical problems common to all religions. These thinkers recognize that human morality and human ideals thrive only when set in a context of a transcendent attitude toward religion and that by pointing to the ground of identity and the common nature of being in the religious experience of man, the essential nature of religion may be defined. Thus, they are committed to reevaluate the meaning of everlastingness, an experience which has been lost and which is the content of that *visio Dei* constituting the structure of all religions. It is the many absorbed everlastingly into the ultimate unity, a unity subsuming what Whitehead calls the fluency of God and the everlastingness of passing experience.

These volumes seek to show that the unity of which we speak consists in a certitude emanating from the nature of man who seeks God and the nature of God who seeks man. Such certitude bathes in an intuitive act of cognition, participating in the divine essence and is related to the natural spirituality of intelligence. This is not by any means to say that there is an equivalence of all faiths in the traditional religions of human history. It is, however, to emphasize the distinction between the spiritual and the temporal which all religions acknowledge. For duration of thought is composed of instants superior to time, and is an intuition of the permanence of existence and its metahistorical reality. In fact, the symbol[1] itself found on cover and jacket of each volume of RELIGIOUS PERSPECTIVES is the visible sign or representation of the essence, immediacy, and timelessness of religious experience; the one immutable center, which may be analogically related to Being in pure act, moving with centrifugal and ecumenical necessity outward into the manifold modes, yet simultaneously, with dynamic centripetal power and with full intentional energy, returning to the source. Through the very diversity of its authors, the Series shows that the basic and poignant concern of every faith is to point to, and overcome the crisis in our apocalyptic epoch—the crisis of man's separation from man and of man's separation from God—the failure of love. The authors endeavor, moreover, to illustrate the truth that the human heart is able, and even yearns, to go to the very lengths of God; that the darkness and cold, the frozen spiritual misery of recent times, are breaking, cracking, and beginning to move, yielding to efforts to overcome spiritual muteness and moral paralysis. In this way, it is hoped, the immediacy of pain and sorrow, the primacy of tragedy and suffering in human life, may be transmuted into a spiritual and moral triumph. For the uniqueness of man lies in his capacity for self-transcendence.

RELIGIOUS PERSPECTIVES is therefore an effort to explore the *meaning* of God, an exploration which constitutes an aspect of man's intrinsic nature, part of his ontological substance. This Series grows out of an abiding concern that in spite of the release of man's creative energy which science has in part accomplished, this very science has overturned the essential order of nature. Shrewd as man's calculations have become concerning his means, his choice of ends which was formerly correlated with belief in God, with absolute criteria of conduct, has become witless. God is not to be treated as an exception to metaphysical principles,

[1] From the original design by Leo Katz.

invoked to prevent their collapse. He is rather their chief exemplification, the source of all potentiality. The personal reality of freedom and providence, of will and conscience, may demonstrate that "he who knows" commands a depth of consciousness inaccessible to the profane man, and is capable of that transfiguration which prevents the twisting of all good to ignominy. This religious content of experience is not within the province of science to bestow; it corrects the error of treating the scientific account as if it were itself metaphysical or religious; it challenges the tendency to make a religion of science—or a science of religion— a dogmatic act which destroys the moral dynamic of man. Indeed, many men of science are confronted with unexpected implications of their own thought and are beginning to accept, for instance, the trans-spatial and trans-temporal dimension in the nature of reality.

RELIGIOUS PERSPECTIVES attempts to show the fallacy of the apparent irrelevance of God in history. This Series submits that no convincing image of man can arise, in spite of the many ways in which human thought has tried to reach it, without a philosophy of human nature and human freedom which does not exclude God. This image of *Homo cum Deo* implies the highest conceivable freedom, the freedom to step into the very fabric of the universe, a new formula for man's collaboration with the creative process and the only one which is able to protect man from the terror of existence. This image implies further that the mind and conscience are capable of making genuine discriminations and thereby may reconcile the serious tensions between the secular and religious, the profane and sacred. The idea of the sacred lies in what it *is,* timeless existence. By emphasizing timeless existence against reason as a reality, we are liberated, in our communion with the eternal, from the otherwise unbreakable rule of "before and after." Then we are able to admit that all forms, all symbols in religions, by their negation of error and their affirmation of the actuality of truth, make it possible to experience that *knowing* which is above knowledge, and that dynamic passage of the universe to unending unity.

God is here interpreted not as a heteronomous being issuing commandments but as the *Tatt-Twam-Asi:* "Do unto others as you would have others do unto you. For I am the Lord." This does not mean a commandment from on high but rather a self-realization through "the other", since the isolated individual is unthinkable and meaningless. Man becomes man by recognizing his true nature as a creature capable of will and decision. For then the divine and the sacred become manifest. And though he believes in choices, he is no Utopian expecting the "coming of the kingdom." Man, individually and collectively, is losing the chains which have bound him to the inexorable demands of nature. The constraints are diminishing and an infinity of choices becomes available to him. Thus man himself, from the sources of his ontological being, at last must decide what is the *bonum et malum*. And though the anonymous forces which in the past have set the constraints do indeed threaten him with total anarchy and with perhaps a worse tyranny than he experienced in past history, he nevertheless begins to see that preceding the moral issue is the cognitive problem: the perception of those conditions for life which permit mankind to fulfill itself and to accept the truth that beyond scientific, discursive knowledge there is non-discursive, intuitive awareness. And, I suggest, this is not to secularize God but rather to gather him into the heart of the nature of matter and indeed of life itself.

The volumes in this Series seek to challenge the crisis which separates, to make reasonable a religion that binds, and to present the numinous reality within the experience of man. Insofar as the Series succeeds in this quest, it will direct mankind toward a reality that is eternal and away from a preoccupation with that which is illusory and ephemeral.

For man is now confronted with his burden and his greatness: "He calleth to me, Watchman, what of the night? Watchman, what of the night?"[2] Perhaps the anguish in the human soul may be assuaged by the answer, by the *assimilation* of the person in God: "The morning cometh, and also the night: if ye will inquire, inquire ye: return, come."[3]

RUTH NANDA ANSHEN

2 Isaiah 21:11.
3 Isaiah 21:12.

PREFACE

MOST OF the translators' prefaces that I have read contain essentially the same things. The translators acknowledge that they have done their best and are indebted to the author for helpful suggestions, adding that the blame for errors which remain is to be laid at their door. I can say nothing other.

But I must say more, for two reasons. First, I am deeply indebted to Professor Oscar Cullmann for his patience in reading and making manifold additions and corrections to the longest article in this collection. I am only sorry that he is so busy that it was impossible for him to go over every article as carefully, but he is constantly busy and could give no more time. Therefore, truly said, the remaining errors are mine.

Second, I am indebted to two other translators who dealt with articles in French. Faith E. Burgess is the wife of a former student of Professor Cullman's; in fact her husband translated the book, *Message to Catholics and Protestants*. She is a graduate of Wellesley College and a candidate for the Doctor of Philosophy degree from the University of Basel. Besides studying in Basel, she has attended classes in two German universities, Tübingen and Heidelberg. Recently she contributed an article to the journal *Dialog* (vol. 5, 1966, pp. 188ff.) entitled "The Declaration on Religious Freedom." Thus she is conversant with Professor Cullmann's thinking and Catholic theology. Mr. Carl Schneider was Professor Cullmann's graduate assistant at Union Theological Seminary, New York, during the fall term, 1966. In that capacity he translated from French Professor Cullmann's inaugural address at Union which appeared in the Winter, 1966, issue of the *Union Seminary Quarterly Review*. He is a graduate of Albright College (1963, B.A. *summa cum laude*) in Reading, Pennsylvania, and is a Danforth Graduate Fellow. At present he is a candidate for the Bachelor of Divinity degree at Union Seminary, and upon completion of his degree in June, 1967, he hopes to pursue doctoral studies in religion. He has traveled in both Europe and Africa and has been involved in ecumenical activities. I alone am responsible for the translation from German.

But allow me to go on and say even more. The translator's job is essentially a thankless one. He is faced with the almost insurmountable task not just of rendering French or German words into English but of knowing so well what the author is saying that he can depart from wooden literalness and yet remain faithful to the sense. And *no one* is satisfied with the result! One author has even demanded that in order to argue with him concerning his interpretation of Barth, one must not use the English, but the German, edition. Evidently thousands of readers are being duped by the translation!

To those who read this translation and find it inadequate, I take full responsibility and fully agree with them. But let me offer one insight: unfortunately this is the only collection of Professor Cullmann's previously unpublished Vatican II articles that I know of, and while it may be a poor representative, it is, nevertheless, *the* representative.

A word of explanation about the plan of the book: if anyone wants to get Professor Cullmann's most developed statement on Vatican Council II, he should turn to the chapter entitled "The Reform of Vatican Council II in the Light of the History of the Catholic Church." The other articles represent discussions of specific points which may be only lightly touched on in that article. Nevertheless, to ignore the shorter chapters is to ignore pieces of a mosaic, steps in a development of thinking concerning the Council, and thereby to invite a less adequate understanding of the whole thought. Introductions have been added to each chapter, detailing where the materials have appeared previously, what the thesis is generally, and who has translated them from what language. I have added throughout coordinating footnotes. That is to say, each article has been cross referenced to other articles in the collection and other books by Professor Cullmann which contain relevant discussions. It is hoped that this will give the reader the optimum opportunity for understanding Professor Cullmann's thinking.

There are few New Testament scholars who are so widely respected in Protestant and Catholic circles as Professor Cullmann. Indeed there are few New Testament scholars who have accomplished what he has by entering into the ecumenical dialogue, for he has put his theology where his life is. He has not developed a theological position which is perfect in theory, irrelevant in life. On the contrary, every day he sees the manifold implications of salvation history for the life of the Church. This volume contains but a glimpse of what must ultimately become a vista of possibilities. We who have translated it are humbly grateful for being even mechanically involved in sharing these insights.

Finally this: I must thank the library staff of California Baptist Theological Seminary for patiently helping me hunt down and clarify obscure references to articles, etc., in Professor Cullmann's manuscripts, and in general providing much bibliographical help. And I must thank Dr. Robert Laurin for those times when he helped me unravel the mysteries of the German idiom and forced me to think "auf Englisch."

JAMES D. HESTER

Covina
New Year's, 1967

I

Foundations: The Theology of
Salvation History and the
Ecumenical Dialogue

*This material was presented as a lecture before many bishops and
cardinals in the Church of St. Louis des Français in Rome during
the third session of Vatican Council II. It was also used when
Professor Cullmann was in the United States in the early months
of 1964. At that time it was translated from a handwritten French
manuscript by Faith E. Burgess. It is included in this collection
because it outlines Professor Cullmann's theological approach to
ecumenism. Here he is careful to point out that salvation history
properly understood provides one of the basic theological foundations upon which ecumenical dialogue can take place. In contrast
to some other theological positions, and contrary to criticisms of
the theology of salvation history as being irrelevant, Professor
Cullmann argues that salvation history is intensely pragmatic.
Using the common ground of God's saving acts in history, ecumenical dialogue has a better chance of being fruitful.*

DURING THE AUDIENCE for the observers at the second session of
Vatican Council II, Pope Paul VI declared that he fully subscribes
to a concrete, historical theology centered on salvation history.
He stated moreover that he would encourage studies directed
toward this end, either at one of the existing institutions or at a
specially created institution, should that be necessary. We rejoice
that the head of the Catholic Church also considers a concrete
theology of salvation history particularly appropriate to serve as
the basis of the ecumenical dialogue.

I would like to concur that a theology of salvation history greatly facilitates this dialogue. We discovered this during the discussions which were organized for the observers each week by the Secretariat for Promoting Unity. As soon as we began to use salvation history in our discussions on the Schemata "De Ecclesia" and "De Oecumenismo," we were speaking the same language— a language which expresses a dynamic, nonstatic conception of the biblical message. Conversely, I believe that all theology which tries to eliminate salvation history destroys the common basis of the ecumenical dialogue.

My main purpose here is not a polemic against that Protestant school of theology which follows the great German theologian Rudolf Bultmann. This school wishes to eliminate salvation history itself, claiming it to be part of biblical mythology. There are, of course, correct elements in their description of the individual act of faith. But while expressing positively the principles of that salvation history which is absolutely essential for all Christian theology, we cannot avoid pointing out the dangers of the so-called existential exegesis which the Bultmannites propagate by using Heidegger's philosophy. We shall not examine the exegetical principles of this school in detail; rather, we shall confine ourselves to recalling that which is important for our specific subject. By means of this philosophical system, this school destroys the distinction between subject and object; it claims that only Heidegger's philosophy can be applied to the interpretation of the New Testament. As a consequence it designates as saving events only the moments when one *encounters* the biblical message. Thus salvation is not made up of unique events, independent of the individual's faith, but only of the *encounter* between the biblical message, the kerygma (the word is preferred by this school), and the individual.

It is evident that as a result of these premises, this school is forced to discard the events of salvation history. Salvation history, they teach, is essential neither for understanding Jesus nor for understanding the Pauline epistles, nor above all for understanding the Gospel of John. John's Gospel eliminated the last traces of salvation history. Salvation history is found only in those books of the New Testament where early Catholicism is already present, notably in Luke's two writings and certain non-Pauline epistles. By creating salvation history, these authors were unfaithful to the biblical message. They were trying solely to overcome a crisis which arose at the moment when they realized that the Kingdom of God, which they had thought to be at hand, had not yet come. Therefore, they invented salvation history by inserting between the past and the future an intermediate period, the period of the Church. Since this period is of indefinite length, it solves the problem of the delay of Christ's return. Thus the idea of salvation history disfigures the Gospel. This school even doubts whether the principal sources of salvation history, Luke's writings, belong in the canon. And in one of his lectures a partisan of this school has gone so far as to speak to students of the "error which Luke and Cullmann have in common!"

Although I reject this negative evaluation of salvation history, I would not keep you from studying the writings of the Bultmannites. Not a false conservatism, but a deep exegetical concern impels me to tell you what the history of salvation revealed in the Bible means, and to warn you how dangerous this school is for the Christian Church and for the ecumenical dialogue.

First of all, even though the Bultmannites consider faith to be the only "event of salvation," when the authors of the New Testament (especially St. Paul) speak of faith, they distinguish clearly within the work of salvation between events and their appropriation by faith. Is it not Paul's great theme that *to believe* means simply to believe that God has accomplished the work for me, the individual—but *for* me precisely *because* it is entirely *independent* of me, independent even of my faith? Certainly I must appropriate this faith. Bultmann is correct when he stresses that when I am confronted by God's work of salvation I am compelled to decide. But this is not a vague decision for what Bultmann calls "that which is not at my disposal." It is a decision *to integrate my existence* into salvation history at the precise point where God has placed me. For this reason it seems completely false to me to play salvation history off against Christian existence. According to the New Testament, Christian existence is impossible unless I believe in a history of salvation independent of me but into which I integrate myself through faith. To object that salvation history is founded on static ("essentialist") thought is false. On the contrary, salvation history is the boldest expression of the prophetic dynamic quality of the Bible. Salvation history is not, as someone has said, a "cemetery" or a "heap of ruins," interesting only to archaeologists and professional historians. It is very relevant. It is a mistake to believe that the biblical message is relevant only when it has been stripped of salvation history. Salvation history is the very heart of the biblical message. The Bible ceases to be a dead letter precisely when we know we are united to the great events of which it speaks by means of salvation history, a history of salvation which attained its pinnacle in Christ and is summed up in Him, but unfolds in the present time in which we live. By faith we place ourselves within this great stream which connects us to the past and to the future. Salvation history makes the events of the past and of the future pertinent just because these events make our intermediate period into salvation history.

While studying the role of salvation history in the New Testament, you will discover how relevant it is. The immense joy, the great peace, and the ardent missionary zeal which filled the early Christians can be explained only by the fact that they were conscious of being coworkers with Christ; they must continue the work which God had begun by choosing the people elected to save humanity and by fulfilling the role of this people in Jesus Christ.

One might object that in speaking of salvation history I am using a concept which is foreign to the New Testament. Thus I would be doing the same thing as those whom I criticize for bringing foreign philosophical concepts to the New Testament. It is true that the term "salvation history" is not to be found in the New Testament. But the idea is there; it is the basis of all biblical revelation and not merely one thing among others. There is a biblical term which very closely approximates salvation history: οἰκονομία. To be sure, this term emphasizes more the idea of a divine *plan* than that of *development*. But it presupposes, nevertheless, that this plan unfolds itself in history. Another biblical term which is often found together with οἰκονομία is μυστήριον. As soon as the apostle Paul speaks of the plan of salvation, he feels compelled to use the word μυστήριον. He uses this word when he speaks of the role with which he knows he is charged as the apostle to the Gentiles (Col., Eph.), or of the panorama of the conversion of the Gentiles and the Jews (Rom. 9-11), or of the final destiny of those who die in Christ (I Cor. 15): "Behold, I tell you a mystery. . . ."

W can deal here only with the essential aspects of the problem. We shall group them around the following points: (1) the relation between the event and its interpretation in salvation history; (2) the relation between salvation history and general history; (3) the role of the present in salvation history; (4) the role of the present in *postbiblical* salvation history.

1. EVENT AND REVELATION IN SALVATION HISTORY

When we say salvation history, we say that God works salvation for us. In other words, through a series of events He saves us from sin and from its consequence, death. But for us these events mean nothing in themselves without the divine revelation about them. This revelation was given by the Holy Spirit to the prophets in the Old Testament, to the apostles in the New Testament, and through them it has been transmitted to us. I want to underscore the fact that revelation *about* the events is a real part of salvation history. Thus salvation history is made up of two elements: the events of salvation themselves and revelation about these events. We must not neglect either the one or the other. The Bultmannites neglect the events. It is false to pose the whole question which has been debated in recent years as if it were a dilemma: either the event or the kerygma (or let us say: the Word which is revelation). In the Bible, the divine Word is both the event and the divine message about the event. In Hebrew, *dabar* (especially in its plural, *debarim*) means "word" and "history." In the prologue to John's Gospel, Jesus Christ, the God who acts and who sums up all salvation history, is called Logos, the Word. It is absolutely futile to ask if the event or the Word came first. In God the two are one. But in the Bible the event is generally prior to the revelation by which the divine interpretation of this event is given to the prophets and the apostles. It is necessary to have both. This is why the prophets and the apostles had to be at one and the same time *eyewitnesses* of an event which was external to them and *bearers* of a revelation about this event. From beginning to end, salvation history unfolds in this manner. The prophet in the Old Testament and the apostle in the New Testament take part, therefore, in salvation history. In his theology of the Old Testament, Gerhard von Rad shows how the whole history of Israel unfolds by means of this combination of event, its interpretation, then new events and the reinterpretation of salvation history in the light of these new events. The combination of events, their interpretation and continual reinterpretation, constitutes salvation history. In the New Testament it is also necessary to have both the event and the revelation which tells me that this is a divine event. Let us take but one example: the discovery of the empty tomb and the appearances of Christ. These events are necessary. But in themselves they do not prove the resurrection of Christ. The New Testament already tells us of one possible interpretation by an unbeliever: the body of Christ may have been stolen; the appearances could be interpreted as psychic phenomena. It was necessary to have divine revelation about these events: the Lord has risen in the flesh.

Since the kerygma deals with *events* which take place independently of us, the New Testament insists on the necessity of *eyewitnesses*. We are all witnesses to the resurrection of Christ, but the apostle must be an eyewitness of these events. Have I not *seen* the Lord? writes the apostle Paul. And the oldest creed, 1 Cor. 15:3, lists the eyewitnesses in order. John's whole Gospel shows that it is a question of two things: *to see* and *to believe*. And the first epistle of John appeals to our senses: "That which we have heard, which we have seen with our eyes, which we have looked upon and touched with our hands . . ." (1 John 1:1). But since we cannot be eyewitnesses any more, but only witnesses, must we not, as someone has proposed, be satisfied with the message without being concerned about knowing the events?

In reality, there are these two aspects: the event and the re-

vealed interpretation about the event. These two make up salvation history. Therefore, in order to try to reconstruct how the
early Christians experienced the faith, we as biblical exegetes
must attempt to recover both the event itself and the revelation
about the event. That is the hermeneutical problem as it is posed
by the New Testament. Exegesis, therefore, has two phases, which,
nevertheless, must never be isolated from one another. Since salvation history is a series of events centered in Christ, and God
has revealed their meaning to the prophets and to the apostles,
the interpreter must use all the historical, philogical, and ar-
chaeological tools at his disposal to reconstruct the *event*. At the
same time, however, he must hear the *testimony of faith* which
these same witnesses to the events communicate to us. But let us
emphasize once more that this faith concerns an event and even a
series of events. Faith tells me that they have taken place independently of me, yet for me. This brings us to our second question.

2. SALVATION HISTORY AND GENERAL HISTORY

The whole central section of salvation history is related to
events which have taken place in general history. The incarnation is the climax of general history and gives general history its
meaning, and these events which are related to the incarnate
Christ take place within the framework of general history. They
are inextricably bound together with other historical events, the
history of Israel, the people of God. And extending beyond the
history of Israel, they are also bound to *historically nonverifiable*
events, the events of creation and the events at the end. Through
this connection salvation history already distinguishes itself from
general history. If by definition the events of creation and the
end are unverifiable from the historical point of view, this is
not to say that it is not essential that they are *events*. To be sure,
in Genesis salvation history does use mythological elements found
in other religions in order to speak of creation. But by having
united these mythological elements with that central part of
salvation history which is composed of historically verifiable
events, the biblical authors have already demythologized these

events. In the Old Testament, creation is connected with the history of Israel, with the exodus. In the prologue of John's Gospel it is connected with the events of the life of Jesus and even with John the Baptist. These historically nonverifiable events are seen entirely in the light of the historical events of salvation history. Certainly we must distinguish between historically nonverifiable events and historically verifiable events. We must not treat the events of creation as though they were historical events in the usual sense. But their very essence is event, divine action. Those who demythologize do not do justice to the intention of the biblical narratives in Genesis when they try to explain the profound meaning of these narratives as the expression of a summons to understand human existence in a certain fashion. Such perhaps is the sense of myth *outside* the Bible. *Within* the Bible, myths are *historicized*. Their exact meaning is indicated by their *connection* with the historical part of the Bible. This shows their character as divine *event* situated clearly outside the historical sphere but bound to the historical sphere. One must not remove this character of *event* from them. When, under the pretext of demythologizing, someone interprets the histories of creation not as events but as expressions of the situation of human existence, he relapses into the sense that myth has *outside* the Bible. He re-mythologizes what in fact the Bible has demythologized. I hope to return to these questions later in a study of the role of creation in the New Testament.

It is, therefore, characteristic for salvation history to combine historically verifiable events with historically nonverifiable events. But the central part of salvation history is made up of a series of historically verifiable events. What is the connection between this central part of salvation history and general history? We shall deal with what salvation history has in common with general history and then how it is different. Most objections to salvation history are based on a misconception; they assume that salvation history is inspired by Hegel and that there is no difference at all between general history and salvation history.

To begin with, how do they correspond? (*a*) Salvation history, like general history, is a series of successive events (*b*) The great events of salvation, although they are explained by faith as *divine* events, all belong within the *framework of history*. This is true both in the Old Testament, where salvation history is presented as the history of the people of Israel, and in the New Testament, where it deals first with the life of Jesus and then with the life of a small community. Again and again the New Testament reminds us that this special history is unfolded within the framework of secular history: Herod the Great, his sons and successors, the Roman empire, Emperor Augustus, the census, Tiberius, the Roman procurators, Pontius Pilate, Felix, Festus, Proconsul Gallio. All of these items are mentioned only incidentally, but they suffice to remind us that the events of salvation history occur within the framework of history, although for the professional historian these events are insignificant or nonexistent. Salvation history, therefore, is not history separated from general history but within general history.

But as soon as we examine this series of events more closely, we discover a fundamental difference: salvation history is not continuous in a chronological sense as general history is. Obviously from God's point of view all history, even so-called secular history, is under divine sovereignty, and in this way all history is connected with salvation history. This point is basic to our whole discussion. But the Bible speaks to us of a particular history, of a history of salvation which gives its meaning to general history. According to it, God has chosen particular events: first a particular nation, then (at the climax) the life of the incarnate Lord, then a small community through which the return to all mankind takes place. God has chosen only certain events; they follow one another, but the continuity is often interrupted by larger or smaller chronological gaps. The period between the last Old Testament prophet and John the Baptist is one of these gaps. Certainly there are bonds which also link the events of this period to salvation history. One may even find here some very important elements which prepare for the history of the New Testament (such as Qumran). But as such they are not included in the divine choice.

Besides choice, there is another factor: God has connected the various events chosen by Him. They have been connected according to God's plan, which is focused on Christ. Therefore, this is not a philosophy of hisory, even though there is a certain analogy. For God can only reveal this divine plan, and man can only believe and understand it through the Holy Spirit. This is precisely the "mystery" revealed to the prophets and the apostles. The principle of this history of salvation is thus the election of a minority for the salvation of the totality. Whoever does not understand this principle cannot understand anything of salvation history. Those who are unable to comprehend that the fourth chapter of the Schema "De Oecumenismo" speaks of the Jews in a different manner from other peoples or religions have simply not understood this principle of election. The particular role reserved for the Jews is self-evident only in the light of salvation history and in the context of salvation history. Outside this context there would be no reason to distinguish between Judaism and other religions.

Election is necessary because of man's sin. For sin, man's revolt, is not only the cause of God's plan of salvation, but continues to oppose salvation history. That is why salvation history is characterized both by the *continuity* of the divine plan and by historical *contingency*. To elect a people does not mean that this people has been given an advantage in *salvation* compared to the rest of humanity, but that this people has to fulfill a particular *mission* to be a witness to the world. This is also important for the idea of the Church. Salvation history is directed toward the whole of humanity. We must not overlook this essential point. Salvation history is perpetually concerned with all the nations and religions of mankind. As a consequence, they are also the concern of the Church. It is always necessary, therefore, to consider the two aspects of salvation history: *the whole of humanity as its objective and constant concern, the election of the minority as the means.* Those who neglect the first aspect end in a sectarianism foreign to the Bible. Those who neglect the second aspect end in a syncretism equally foreign to the Bible. Before Christ came, salvation history narrowed progressively: creation—mankind— the people of Israel—the remnant of Israel, and the reduction

continued: the Servant of Yahweh—the Unique One, Christ, rep-
resenting the remnant of the people of Israel and the whole of
mankind. Here salvation history has arrived at its turning point:
an individual who substitutes Himself for all, who sums up all
past salvation history and who already includes in Himself future
salvation history. After Christ there is the reverse movement, a
progressive expansion which continues to follow the principle of
election: Christ—the Twelve—the small Judeo-Christian community—the Church of the Jews and Gentiles—mankind—the
new creation.

The more that election, at the first glance, appears to remove
us from universal history, the more, on the contrary, this reduc-
tion applies to universal history. Thus it is precisely through the
One, the εἰς of which Gal. 3:16 speaks, that all men are saved;
yet the progressive expansion remains centered on the One, Jesus
Christ. During His life Christ limits both His preaching and the
preaching of the Twelve to the lost sheep of the house of Israel:
"Go nowhere among the Gentiles, and enter no town of the
Samaritans, but go rather to the lost sheep of the house of Israel"
(Matt. 10:5). Does this mean that Jesus is not interested in all
men, in the Gentiles? On the contrary, He wants the disciples to
limit themselves at first to the house of Israel in order to conform
to the plan of salvation. Then later, after His death and resurrection, they will be all the better prepared to preach to the
Gentiles. In his panorama of history in Rom. 9-11, the apostle
Paul shows how the principle of election continues in salvation
history until the end of time, until the moment when it arrives
at its goal and is combined with the history of mankind. Yet salvation history is not absorbed by world history; rather, the history
of the world will be absorbed by salvation history.

As salvation history unfolds, the center in Christ and the final
goal are never lost from view. It is true that the New Testament
itself does not draw out the indirect lines which pointed the
peoples of antiquity toward salvation history. However, the book
of Acts (14:16) mentions the nations whom God left to follow
their own ways. In the discourse on Mars Hill (Acts 17:26) Paul
says that God fixed for the nations their allotted times and the

limits of their habitation. Through Christ's revelation one could try to draw out this idea and to recover in the history of the nations the hidden ways which prepared them for salvation history. But such an endeavor would have to be controlled by the center of salvation history. One could write a history of religions from this point of view. However, no one since Justin Martyr, and the other apologists of the second century has attempted this very difficult task. What I wish to show is that salvation history, in spite of its concentration or, rather, precisely *because of it*, does not exclude universal history. Salvation history is perpetually connected to world history. We must remember this in order to understand the role which our *present time* plays in salvation history. This leads us to the third part of this brief exposition, to the very heart of our subject.

3. THE ROLE OF OUR PRESENT TIME IN SALVATION HISTORY

Seen from the perspective of salvation history, our present time is the intermediate period between the resurrection of Christ and His return. The New Testament tells us of our time in its first phase, the time of the apostles; this is extremely important in order to show how salvation history is "relevant." Naturally our postapostolic age must not be simply identified with the time of the apostles. Although the apostolic age is part of the period of the Church, it is still, on the other hand, part of the time of the incarnation. For the apostles are eyewitnesses, which can never be true of other witnesses. The intermediate period implies that the turning point has already been reached, yet the final act is still to come. Permit me to repeat the example which I often use to describe this situation (naturally every example is imperfect): the decisive battle has already taken place, the victory is assured, but the treaty has not yet been signed. In Christ we already have a foretaste of the Kingdom of God, but the old framework remains: death is conquered, but men still die; sin is conquered, but we still sin. We are still waiting for the final victory over death—the resurrection of the body and the new creation. There is a tension between "already" and "not yet." This tension indicates to us that salvation history continues, although that which we are still waiting for is merely the unfolding of what has already been accomplished in Christ. Therefore, salvation history does not cease between Christ's resurrection and His return. This is not one of those chronological gaps in salvation history which we have mentioned. *It is not possible to have such gaps after the coming of Christ when all history becomes salvation history.*

When Jesus Christ came, salvation history took a great step forward, much greater than through the normal progress of time. This principle is basic. We have entered the *final* phase, no matter how long it lasts. We do not know how long it will last. We do know that at the beginning the first Christians expected the end in the immediate future, whereas later they reckoned more and more with a longer duration. This fact cannot be contested, and no one today disagrees with it, but it leaves just enough room for a massive attack leveled against New Testament salvation history.

These critics claim that salvation history was created simply to solve the crisis arising from the delay of the parousia. The whole intermediate period with the tension between "already" and "not yet" was invented after the fact in order to overcome the crisis which developed when the early church realized the Kingdom was not coming immediately. Those who invented salvation history sought to quiet impatient Christians by interjecting the intermediate period of the Church, where the Holy Spirit, the "first fruits" and "down payment" of the final end, was already at work. Above all, by affirming that this intermediate period would last indefinitely, they wanted to reassure all believers. It was mainly Luke who fabricated this makeshift solution. But for Jesus, St. Paul, and John's Gospel, salvation history did not play any role at all. For them it was not essential that history continue. They understood time in the vertical sense and not in the horizontal sense of salvation history. Salvation history was repudiated by the simple fact that the Kingdom of God had not yet come. They eliminated salvation history from the whole Old Testament and interpreted eschatological time in the existential, not the temporal, sense. Temporal eschatology, says Bultmann, is repudiated by the fact that the world continues and "every sane man knows that it will always continue" (in the age of nuclear power this affirmation seems somewhat problematic as far as man is concerned). Thus by inventing salvation history, Luke introduced an intermediate period, the period of the Church, a false solution, false because it is contrary to Jesus' intention and Paul's intention. Someone has even suggested eliminating from the canon not only the two books of Luke but also the other writings which have this view of salvation history (and which for this reason have been described by the rather vague term, "early catholic"). But I am convinced that the critics of salvation history whom we have been describing introduce an arbitrary distinction into the study of the New Testament and also destroy the very basis of the ecumenical dialogue.

It is especially their distinction between Jesus, St. Paul, and the Gospel of John, on the one hand, and Luke, on the other, which is based on false exegesis. Certainly Luke is the one who developed salvation history in detail. But I believe I can show that he is not the first to use a history of salvation in which the present, intermediate period has an important role. There is not a break between Jesus, St. Paul, and the Gospel of John, on the one hand, and Luke and the other epistles, on the other; there is development. Biblical history unfolds. It is true that the first Christians expected the intermediate period to be short, whereas later (already in Luke) it was greatly lengthened. But this is not the crucial point. The important factor is that in the teachings of Jesus as well as in Paul and John there is actually a *present* period, however short it may be. These men already thought of an intermediate period which was characterized by the tension between "already" and "not yet" and which was important because it was connected to the final end. Albert Schweitzer, who claims that for Jesus the Kingdom will come only in the future, is forced to reject all the sayings according to which the Kingdom is present; vice versa, C. H. Dodd, who claims that for Jesus the Kingdom is only present (fully "realized"), has to reject all the sayings according to which the Kingdom will come only in the future. It is obvious that this method of simply rejecting portions of the New Testament is very questionable. In fact there are two elements in Jesus' teaching: since He who is called to bring the future Kingdom is already on earth, He knows that in His person the Kingdom has already come: "the blind receive their sight and the lame walk, lepers are cleansed and the deaf hear, and the dead are raised up" (Matt. 11:5). And further: "But if it is by the Spirit of God that I cast out demons, then the Kingdom of God has come upon you" (Matt. 12:28). And again: "I saw Satan fall like lightning from the heaven" (Luke 10:18). But Jesus speaks at the same time also of the Kingdom which will come in the future: "Thy Kingdom come" (Matt. 6:10). Thus Jesus lived already in the same tension. It is this new factor which separates Jesus from Judaism. For Jesus the intermediate period is also very important in the plan of salvation. Otherwise, why did he talk about ethics in the Sermon on the Mount?

As soon as tension exists between the present and the future, there is salvation history; there is an intermediate period. Throughout Jesus' teaching there is the idea that He sums up past salvation history. Space does not permit me to show that the same is true for St. Paul, and above all for the Gospel of John. Some have falsely used John's Gospel to support the elimination of salvation history. On the contrary, the Gospel of John is a life of Jesus seen entirely from the perspective of salvation history.

The fact that much later the Christians thought the intermediate period would be longer does not mean that they had developed a theory to explain the delay of the parousia. We have seen that already in the Old Testament, salvation history and the revelation about salvation history always unfolds and clarify themselves by means of new events, without, however, losing the constant of the divine plan. The same is true for the development of salvation history in the early church. Here again new events occurred and their meaning was revealed. What were these events? The phenomena of the Holy Spirit, the great miracles of healing experienced daily in the community; the *koinonia*, the communal holding of goods realized by the power of the Holy Spirit as they broke bread together—all these experiences revealed to the Christians that the end had already begun; they

made clear that the Holy Spirit and the Church were eschatological realities, a foretaste of the end. These are the events which
convinced them that this period (which is already the final period
although the end was still to come) might last considerably longer,
and that neither impatience nor eschatological fever were justified. Because of these events in the early church, there was an
entirely normal development of salvation history. Whether the
time would be short or long, this did not change the *plan* of
salvation, because in any case there was the intermediate period
from the beginning. There is, therefore, no break between Jesus
and Paul, on the one hand, and Luke, on the other.

The supposed "serious crisis" caused by the fact that the Kingdom of God was delayed could never occur as long as the Christians experienced every day that the decisive events—the Holy
Spirit, the communion with the risen Christ—had already taken
place. It is not necessary to imagine the first Christians as rabbis
tormenting themselves with the question: How can we solve the
crisis caused by the delay of the parousia? A crisis of this sort
could happen only much later, at the moment when the manifestations of the Holy Spirit began to diminish.

In the age of the New Testament it is neither a theoretical
problem nor a crisis but, rather, their tremendous joy in the Holy
Spirit, their great mission successes, as well as the help they received from the Holy Spirit during persecutions, which revealed
to the Christians that the present age might continue for a longer
time. The Holy Spirit (who is the first fruits, the down payment,
foretaste of the end) was not, as has been claimed, a theological
device invented in order to conceal the fact that the Kingdom had
not yet come. He was a reality experienced every day.

Here again salvation history developed by means of these events.
What is the precise interpretation revealed along with these
events to the early church about the meaning of our time? That it
is the time of the Holy Spirit; it is the time of the Church, the
body of Christ.

Our time is the time of the Holy Spirit! Here we see most
easily that it is an intermediate period, a time of tension between
"already" and "not yet." The end has already begun, although

it is still to come. In Acts when Peter interprets the miracle of Pentecost, he says that it fulfills that which Joel prophesied: in the last days the Holy Spirit will no longer be the exclusive privilege of certain prophets, but everyone in the Church, both young and old, will be seized by Him (Acts 2:17-18). The eighth chapter of the letter to the Romans shows clearly the tension created by the Holy Spirit. This is what the apostle means by the terms "down payment," "first fruits," "foretaste": already! The Holy Spirit is the power of the resurrection. He is the opposite of the power of sin and death. At the time of the resurrection of the dead, He will create new bodies. This future is now; the resurrection is already here, *now*, all is within time. This is the meaning of our time in salvation history. Nevertheless, the Holy Spirit causes us to sigh, says the apostle, because death has not yet disappeared (Rom. 8:26). He is still encumbered by the limits of our carnal existence. He searches for a divine language which will be suitable for Him, "a language of the angels" (1 Cor. 13,), but He is hindered by the imperfect organs of our bodies and only produces the sighs of speaking in tongues (glossolalia). Thus there is a tension, but we know that in principle it is already overcome in Christ.

This time of the Spirit is the time of the Church, the period of salvation history in which we live. This is the basis of the whole ecumenical dialogue. The Church also participates in the tension between "already" and "not yet." She is that which is most divine on this earth because she is the "body of Christ," the body of the risen Christ. And yet the authors of the New Testament knew that nevertheless it was sinful men who made up the body of Christ. Nowhere is the tension more evident than in the Church. Nowhere is the gap so deplorable between that which we are already—the body of Christ—and that which still exists— our sin. It is now more evident what the apostle means when he speaks of the "sighs" of the Holy Spirit. No author in the New Testament omits this tension in the early church. It is false to believe that sin did not exist in the early church. Already in Acts we hear how Ananias and Sapphira sinned (Acts 5), and how there was grumbling about the distribution of alms to the widows (Acts

6). Later we read of the disputes between Paul and Barnabas (Acts 15:36-40) and between Paul and Peter at Antioch (Gal. 2:11-21). The Pauline letters are full of information not only about the marvelous work of the Holy Spirit, but also about those tragic events which witness to the fact that although the Church introduces the Kingdom of God, it (the Church) is not the Kingdom of God.

The dialogue between separated brothers must deal especially with this tension in which the Church exists in order to fulfill her role in the intermediate period. For everything that separates us can be reduced to our way of understanding this tension. Protestants find that in certain points the "not yet" has not been sufficiently respected by the Catholic Church. Catholics, on the other hand, find that Protestants have not recognized the fact that the tension is already "eliminated," abolished in Christ and in His Church; the "already" is not taken seriously enough. Be that as it may, if the basis of our discussion is truly that which the New Testament tells us about salvation history and about the role of our time in salvation history, our dialogue cannot fail to be fruitful. If we destroy our mutual basis in salvation history, I do not see how the dialogue can be profitable.

But as we discuss this tension, we must examine carefully what the New Testament teaches us about the christological aspect of the period in which we live. Christ died and rose again; that is the *center* of all revelation. And He will return at the end. This is another affirmation which concerns time. Has His function ceased during the period in which we live? No, the Gospel of John in its entirety endeavors to show that the same Christ who was incarnate on earth governs His Church and the world at the present time. "I will not leave you desolate" (John 14:8) is the theme of the farewell discourses. In another book I have already shown that it is the real, invisible Lordship of Christ, visible only to faith, which the early Christians proclaimed in their first brief confessions of faith: *Kyrios Christos!* It is necessary to understand what this implies. Later, in the more developed confessions, they say, "seated at the right hand of the Father," "all powers are subjected to Him." They are quoting Psalm 110. It is not by chance that no text of the Old Testament was cited more often by the first Christians than this one; precisely this text expressed what had been revealed to them about the relationship between Christology and the present age. According to the New Testament this is how Christ's victory unfolds within the plan of divine events.

All the creedal formulas which sum up the faith of the first Christians insist on the victory won by Christ over the invisible powers; we find an example of this in Phil. 2: "God has highly exalted Him and bestowed on Him the name which is above every name [Kyrios-Adonai is the name of God Himself] that at this name every knee [of invisible powers] shall bow" (Phil. 2:9-10). These are the same invisible powers which exist behind terrestial governments; they are subjected to Christ and put into His service. But here again it is obvious that the present age is the time of *tension* between "already" and "not yet." These powers are already subject to Christ, and yet they must still be conquered at the end of time.

Invisibly Christ governs the universe and the world. I often describe this Lordship by a diagram made up of two concentric circles. There is a small circle: that is the Church; the large circle around it is the world. Their common center is Christ. From the small circle, the body of Christ, He governs the world.

What is it that distinguishes the Lordship of Christ over the world from His rule of the Church? The world *does not know* that it is ruled by Christ, for His dominion is still invisible, visible only to faith. The Church is the community of those who through faith *know* that Christ is Lord. They have not been given any advantage in regard to salvation, since salvation concerns the entire world; but they have the advantage of being conscious members of the Kingdom of Christ in order to testify that we are saved by Christ.

According to the New Testament, what is the precise task which we have in the intermediate period? Does time still continue because we have a definite role to fulfill? Why did the end not come when all was accomplished in Christ? The answer is given to us in the synoptic apocalypse (Mark 13:10; Matt. 24:14): before the end comes, the gospel must be preached to all nations.

That is what drives St. Paul to preach everywhere, to search always for new places. Having finished in the east, he turns toward the west: "Woe to me if I do not preach the Gospel" 1 Cor. 9:16). Along with many other interpreters, I consider it probable that in Rev. 6:2 the first horseman who comes is not, like the other three, one of the plagues. Rather, he is the victorious proclamation preceding the final plagues. In Acts 1:6 the disciples asked the risen Christ, "Will you at this time restore the Kingdom to Israel?" And the Lord replied, "It is not for you to know the day or the hour, but you will receive the Holy Spirit, and He will enable you to preach the gospel even to the ends of the earth." The purpose of our age is, therefore, *to preach,* to witness to the world through the Word and through our lives. The task of the Church is to bear witness to the world.

As a corollary, we each have an individual task. There is an ethic firmly grounded in salvation history, and it is absolutely false to believe that only the existential interpretation of the New Testament includes the call to decision. In every one of its books the New Testament calls us, summons us. The Bultmannites are correct when they insist on this summons (*Anrede*) and on the *decision* of faith. I am in complete agreement with Bultmann when he says that according to the New Testament our situation is characterized by the fact that we are constantly in the state of decision. But the New Testament does not mean this in a sense hostile to salvation history. Not only is the "now," the νῦν, the moment of decision, not opposed to salvation history, as the Bultmannites claim, but the summons, the making of the decision, *presupposes* salvation history. The νῦν of which the New Testament speaks is not the same as the moment of decision in which man "always" exists. No, it is the moment in which we truly exist *now,* in the "now" of the present period of salvation history. The precise meaning of this period within the plan of salvation defines what the summons to decision signifies. And the *decision* is just this: to integrate ourselves into salvation history at the place and at the moment in which we find ourselves. The decision for Christ cannot be a vague decision not to be bound to the things of this world (Bultmann calls such a decision

Entweltlichung). It is, rather, a decision for Him who died and rose and is at the right hand of the Father, ruling invisibly over the Church and over the world until His visible dominion at the end of time.

Thus every person must make a definite decision. What salvation history tells us about the meaning of our age defines that for which we must decide. It is not a question of deciding simply for the sake of deciding independently of an object. It must be a decision to integrate ourselves into the period of salvation history in which we live. (A decision to support Hitler, such as that made by the philosopher Heidegger, the philosopher of decision, in his speech at the convocation of the University of Freiburg in 1934, could not be such a decision.) Some object that salvation history leaves no place for individual decision. To make this objection is to have understood nothing of the basic nature of salvation history. Salvation history describes for us the *plan,* yet within this revelation about the plan of salvation history there is room for historical contingency and for individual decision.

In our discussion of what characterizes the present period of salvation history there is one other important point, the liturgy; in the worship service we re-present the past events of salvation history; we experience the present reality of Christ and His Lordship, and we have a foretaste of the final end.

This whole dynamic movement, this whole stream of events, connects all periods of time and binds us who are within this stream to all the periods of salvation history; all this takes place especially in the liturgy, for in the worship service we are *united* with the center of salvation history, Christ, who sums up all of salvation history. Already in the Old Testament the liturgy was gradually historicized; agrarian festivals became feasts celebrating the great events of the history of Israel, the chosen people (the Passover). In the New Covenant, salvation history continues to unfold; the festival of the Passover is connected to the central event, the death and resurrection of Christ. And the Eucharist not only recalls and re-presents the death of Christ, the Last Supper and the Passover meals, but it also is a foretaste of the future. The eucharistic prayer, *Maranatha,* "Our Lord, come!"

means both "Our Lord, come at the end" and "Our Lord, come now" among us as you were present among the disciples during their meals together after the resurrection. The past, present, and future are combined in one single reality. It is encouraging that in the Schema "De Liturgia" this perspective is not lacking. We have come to the end of this very brief exegetical study of salvation history in the New Testament. But I do not wish to close this study without raising a fourth question.

4. DID SALVATION HISTORY CEASE WITH THE END OF THE APOSTOLIC AGE, AFTER THE EYEWITNESSES OF THE DECISIVE EVENTS HAD DIED?

Is there, so to speak, a chronological gap between the New Testament period and the final end, an end which is also the object of biblical revelation? In following my exposition you have already noticed that this cannot be the case. But what is the connection between biblical salvation history and postbiblical salvation history? The future ecumenical dialogue must deal with this problem. I believe that if we ask the question in this way, the old controversy between Protestants and Catholics about "Scripture and tradition" will take on a new dimension. If we say "biblical salvation history" in the place of "Scripture," the old problem will not disappear, but it will be transformed. For Scripture could not then be considered a "dead letter" but would be seen in its connection with the present age. I am pleased that among Catholic theologians it is precisely Father Danièlou who insists on "salvation history"; we have often discussed the problem of "Scripture and tradition." I believe that what Father Congar calls the *living* tradition should also be understood within the context of salvation history.

Permit me to lay out a few guidelines: certainly salvation history continues. But is it normative in the same way biblical salvation history is normative? What does the formation of the *canon* mean to us? To begin with, it means simply that salvation history is the principle which unites Scripture. The old dispute about the central criterion of Scripture (which has been revived again today by Küng and Käsemann) is settled by the idea of the canon itself. The unity of the Old and New Testaments indicates that salvation history is the unifying factor in the Bible. If anyone chooses another factor, even if it is a doctrine as important as justification by faith (which Käsemann proposes), he makes an arbitrary choice, because he does not safeguard the *unity* of Scripture. The fact that the canon united the Old Testament and the New Testament can mean only that the *unifying principle* must be that which binds the two Testaments: salvation history, centered in Christ. On such an important point we dare not choose whatever criterion we like.

But what is the purpose of the canon? On the one hand (*a*) it shows that *the revelation given by eyewitnesses about the central event, the work of Jesus Christ, has ceased.* The idea of the canon is not an idea invented after the fact, but it is the necessary *result of biblical salvation history.* The idea of the canon arises because the events belonging to the time of the incarnation were considered to be the decisive events of salvation history, after which there could be no more than the *unfolding* of these events. The New Testament contains the idea that apostleship means being an eyewitness of the decisive events. But, on the other hand (*b*) the canon does indicate that salvation history *continues* as the unfolding of the decisive events. We must keep both aspects in mind.

It is extremely important that in the New Testament the apostolic age is part of the period of revelation and that the book of Acts and the epistles are in the canon. For these belong already to the *intermediate period* between the resurrection of Christ and His return; they are the beginning of the same period which continues into the *postbiblical period,* into our age. And the basic characteristics of our postbiblical period are in fact the same as the characteristics of the apostolic age, with one exception, that the eyewitnesses are no longer among us. But in the writings of the New Testament we have their testimony as a norm.

The postbiblical period corresponds to the apostolic age because in its entirety the postbiblical period is the time of the *tension* between "already" and "not yet." It is the period of the Church, of the Holy Spirit, of witnessing to the whole world, of including all mankind. Everything that we have said about that part of the apostolic age between the resurrection of Christ and the final end applies also to our time.

But one difference remains: as far at *our* time is concerned, we do not have an inerrant guide as we have for biblical times to say whether an event was or is salvation history in the special sense we have mentioned. We do not simply say everything that happened in the history of the Church for the past twenty centuries is salvation history in the strictest sense of the word, as can be said of all the events of biblical salvation history. In its teaching office the Catholic Church has an institution which defines tradition—the teaching office determines exactly where salvation history develops. We also recognize that a teaching office is necessary. We disagree only on the infallibility of this teaching office. When the future ecumenical dialogue deals with this question, as it undoubtedly will, the question should be approached from the point of view of salvation history. But having said this, we must keep in mind that both Catholics and Protestants do constantly use the history of salvation contained in the Bible to judge the history of salvation which is unfolded in the Church. In the light of the Bible, in light of the general pattern of the divine plan which it reveals, we examine everything that happens within the Church and outside the Church. For biblical salvation history has taught us that according to God's plan salvation history applies to all men. Therefore, we ought to use the Bible to understand our newspapers. But we must not do this in the same way as the sects; they try to use the Bible to calculate the date of the final end, thus arrogating to themselves the right to know precisely what God has *not* wished to reveal to us ("the day and the hour"). The New Testament expressly forbids us to investigate such matters.

By revealing the plan and direction of salvation history, biblical salvation history assists us in discovering with the aid of the Holy Spirit how salvation history unfolds in the events of our daily lives. However, when we venture to discover how salvation history unfolds, we must remember that in mysterious ways God can also make use of man's sin to execute His plan. Salvation history does not progress in a straight line. Biblical salvation history illustrates how this happens. In Rom. 9-11, Paul points out that even today the Jews remain the chosen people. God has made use of their unbelief in order to draw the Gentiles into salvation history. But the Gentiles have been grafted into the Jewish tree, and at the end Israel "according to the flesh" will be converted. Is not this event a key which enables us to understand the intermediate period? Is not this nation's miraculous preservation in spite of persecutions a witness to the existence of salvation history and to the fact that God has reserved them for the consummation mentioned in Rom. 11? This is the reason why in salvation history and only in salvation history the Jewish people occupy a special place.

God has not revealed the mysterious ways by which He brings good out of evil. Yet does not this example from Rom. 9-11 allow us to discover the hand of God also in our divisions, however serious may be the responsibility of those who in one way or another have caused our divisions? Our sin is great, for we have transformed the diversity of the gifts of the Spirit into divisions. I am not trying to determine which side is at fault. Whoever is at fault, our divisions are caused by sin and are opposed to God's will. Do not these divisions which seem so necessary have their importance for salvation history? Seen in this light, do not our divisions have significance? Should they not have warned us constantly to have more respect for the diversity of the gifts of the Spirit? Do they not call us continually to renewal? On the other hand, this "detour" of salvation history, like the "detour" into unbelief by the chosen people, cannot make us lose sight of the final goal, so often reiterated at the present council: *ut unum sint!* ("that they all may be one"). In the light of biblical salvation history, may we not see that what happens today through the creation of the World Council of Churches and through Vatican Council II is a sign that the "detour," our divisions, shall not last forever? Is not this desire for renewal, for drawing closer together with mutual respect for each other's diversity, a sign that salvation history is advancing? Is this not a sign that in spite of all our imperfections and all our sins God is at work? Thus God even makes use of our divisions to effect a general renewal.

In a similar fashion the existence of non-Christian nations

today fits into the divine plan. It is God's will that we should be confronted with the non-Christian world. We should not think that the existence of non-Christians means that they shall not be saved. But it should remind us that we must continually show them through preaching and our daily lives that we are saved by Christ.

We are conscious of belonging to those who know that Christ *has* saved us, that He reigns, that we are called to be witnesses; in our modest way we are instruments of the divine plan; to be aware of these events is the basis of our Christian existence, of the decision which is mentioned so frequently today. Does it not require a much more daring faith to believe that we are involved in a divine history which concerns me, as an individual, but which concerns me just because it does *not* unfold *only* in my personal encounter with God? Is not the necessary "scandal" of faith the conviction of being integrated into a history which first takes place outside me? We must not believe that it is just because modern science has advanced that salvation history has become a "scandal." Already in antiquity it was a scandal to consider salvation events to be historical events. The Athenians on Mars Hill would not have laughed if Paul had proclaimed a kerygma stripped of salvation history. They laughed precisely because he spoke of the center of salvation history, of its decisive event, the resurrection.

This is why it is so dangerous to want to eliminate the scandal of salvation hitsory; this would remove the very heart of the Bible. Today is not the first time in Christian history that some-one has attempted to discard salvation history; Gnosticism had just such a program. It is true that the philosophy which Christian Gnosticism used to eliminate salvation history from the Christian message was quite different from the one by which some try to get rid of salvation history today. But the purpose was the same.

In order to fit Christianity as well as all other ancient religions into the vast philosophical syncretism of the age, it was necessary to cut out its very core, salvation history. For there was a factor here which rebelled against syncretism. If Gnosticism had triumphed, if it had really been able to discard salvation history in the second century, Christianity would have been swallowed up by philosophical syncretism along with all the other religions of antiquity. They have disappeared. Christianity and Judaism alone resisted. They could resist precisely because both of them are rooted in salvation history. Irenaeus, the greatest theologian of salvation history, understood the fundamental issue in this battle. All the fathers of the second century realized that the very lifeblood of Christian revelation was at stake. (I do not understand how theologians can say that salvation history is nothing but a "cemetery"; on the contrary, a theology based on salvation history frees us from all that is static. It keeps us in constant contact with life, with concrete realities.)

As through the Spirit the apostle Paul comprehends the depth of this revelation, he addresses to God (and precisely at the end of the theology of salvation history he develops in Rom. 9-11) the hymn of praise with which I shall close this chapter: "O the depth of the riches and wisdom and knowledge of God! How unsearchable are His judgments and how inscrutable His ways!" —inscrutable to "human wisdom," yet revealed to the apostle and discernible to that other wisdom, "the wisdom of God" mentioned by him in 1 Cor. 2, where he says that God reveals it to us through the Spirit (1 Cor. 2:10).

II

The New Direction: Divine Revelation
and the Virgin Mary

*These two short articles were translated from French by Carl
Schneider from mimeographed "press releases." Specifically they
have to do with questions to Professor Cullmann concerning the
Council texts on Revelation and Mary. But generally they deal
with a much broader topic, that of the relationship of Scripture
and tradition. This is the fundamental point of disagreement between Protestants and Catholics, and in these interviews Professor Cullmann speaks first to the necessity of Scripture as a
norm for revelation, and second to what happens, using Mariology
as a specific instance, when Scripture is not used as that norm.*

*Professor Cullmann, who followed the Council from its first
session as guest of the Secretariat for Christian Unity, was inter-
viewed by the Press and Information Service of the Federal Council of Churches in Italy on the problem of Scripture and Tradition
posed by the Council on the occasion of the debate over the
schema "De Divina Revelatione" which took place from Septem-
ber 30th to October 6th.*

1. "DE DIVINA REVELATIONE"

The Schema "De Divina Revelatione (Concerning Divine Revelation) is a great improvement over the Schema of two years ago
entitled "De Fontibus Revelationis." The present Schema does
not close the doors to future developments when it says that
Scripture and tradition "are closely connected with one another":

inter se connectuntur. But there is more. There is also an open door when the Schema says that the teaching office serves Scripture: *Magisterium verbum Dei ministrat.* Nevertheless, a point remains which separates us: Scripture is not considered by the Catholics as standing over against, in confrontation with (vis-à-vis), the Church.

While this confrontation (vis-à-vis) did not exist in the apostolic age, it does exist in the postapostolic age. The relation between Scripture and tradition must therefore be defined in a different manner when we are talking about the apostolic tradition from that when we are speaking of the postapostolic tradition. As for the apostolic tradition, I subscribe to the Shema's *inter se connectuntur* and *pari reverentia veneranda est* ("both are to be held in equal reverence"). But this equality does not exist for the postapostolic tradition.[1]

The distinction between the apostolic and the postapostolic is based on the significance which the event of the formation of the canon holds. I am not thinking here of its definitive fixation; I am thinking of the very idea of the canon and its first realizations which we are able to locate about A.D. 150. We know the historical cause of this. It was the time when there was a deluge of apocryphal gospels, and certain of these were playing a larger role in the living traditions of the Church at the beginning of the second century than our canonical Gospels. I am thinking especially of the proto-gospel of James, which was so important for the birth of Mariology.

There was, however, a change in the relation between Scripture and tradition after the formation of the canon.

At the time of the formation of the apostolic tradition, the eyewitnesses, those who confessed this faith, and the representatives of the teaching ministry were one and the same people. Thus we may say that during the apostolic age, tradition, Scripture, and the teaching office were intermingled. On the other hand, since the formation of the canon, the eyewitnesses and those who confess the Christian faith are no longer the same.

[1] See section four of the article "The Theology of Salvation History and the Ecumenical Dialogue," pp. 40 ff.

They are separated. This is the reason that after the apostolic age there exists a "confrontation" of Scripture in relation to the Church. In creating the canon, the Church herself, in an act of humility, acknowledged this fact: henceforth the postapostolic tradition and the postapostolic teaching office are no longer on the same level as Scripture. They are always dependent on each other, and in this sense we are still able to say *inter se connectuntur*. But the three no longer exist on the same level. The postapostolic tradition and the postapostolic teaching office are subject to the norm of the apostolic tradition fixed henceforth in Scripture.[2]

Because of this superior norm, insofar as it is considered a superior norm, a reform is always possible within the Church. This is the importance of the canon for the life of the Church. The Bible is a dynamic norm. On the one hand, it calls forth renewal; on the other, it provides the criterion for distinguishing legitimate development from distortions. In the postapostolic Church and in her living traditions the same Holy Spirit is at work as in the Scripture, but the Holy Spirit is mixed with other spirits and mingled with sources of error. This is why there are also some traditions in the postapostolic traditions of the Church which are contrary to the Bible. As she seeks to discern the true from the false, the postapostolic Church is not herself able to be the judge. It is necessary for her that Scripture stand over against her, a superior norm. If this is not the case, if there is not this confrontation, a great danger exists for the Church: that of self-justification, of considering as authentic traditions all the ecclesiastical traditions which have been fixed and which have triumphed in the course of the centuries. Then she takes recourse to the theory of "truths which are *implicitly* contained in the Bible."[3]

Of course there are truths implicitly contained in the Bible. This is the case with the doctrine of the Trinity. We may say that it is in the Bible only in an implicit form. There are elements in the Bible which lead naturally to the doctrine of the

2 See section two of the article "The Reform of the Second Vatican Council in the Light of the History of the Catholic Church," pp. 76 ff.
3 Compare this with section four, ibid., pp. 96 ff.

Trinity; they give birth to this doctrine. But there are other doctrines in the living tradition of the postapostolic age, such as the bodily assumption of Mary. Because the Bible has not been seen in its role over against the Church as a superior judge, the Catholic Church has placed this conception on the same level as the Trinity, and she has proclaimed that it is a truth implicitly contained in the Bible. In fact, in this case it is not the Bible which has given birth to this doctrine, but justification for this belief was sought in the Bible after the event as a result of this theory of "truths contained *implicitly* in the Bible." Without wishing to affront the faith of the Catholics, it must be said that if the bodily assumption of Mary is implicit in the Bible, it is hard to see what is not implicit in the Bible. In this case the theory of the Catholic conservatives who squarely affirm that the assumption is not in the Bible but in the tradition is to be preferred. But it must be said further that it is a deviant tradition.

The necessity of subjecting the postapostolic traditions to an authority over against it applies also to the postapostolic teaching office. The postapostolic Church has need of a teaching office, but a teaching office subject to the "vis-à-vis" which is Scripture. To be sure, the Bible must be interpreted in the Church, since the same Holy Spirit who inspired Scripture is at work in the Church. But if there is not this subjection, the teaching office becomes a source of error more dangerous than if there were no teaching ministry at all. Has not the present Council implicitly recognized this, since it carefully avoids making new dogmas and making dogmas a norm equal to the norm of Scripture?

What has been said above about the Church not being subject to the Scripture as a standard over against it applies only to Catholic theory. Fortunately the Catholic Church in reality is quite often subjected in practice, and often subjects herself, to the Bible. It ought to be asked if the present Council with its desire for renewal is not inspired, in the last analysis, by a practical subjection to the Bible.[4]

---

[4] For another discussion of this see Cullmann's article in *Dialogue of the Way* (G. Lindbeck, ed.), Minneapolis (1965), "The Bible in the Council," pp. 129-144. The essence of this article is contained in the articles published in this collection.

In the ecumenical context the dialogue about the problem of tradition will progress if from the Protestant side we can recognize the value of the living tradition in the postapostolic church and the value of the teaching office, and if from the Catholic side the confrontation of the Scripture as a superior norm in relation to the Church is acknowledged.

As regards the *sola Scriptura* of the Reformers, I would replace this formula by the formula: *Scriptura, traditio, magisterium, sed Scriptura sola norma superior.*

Finally, attention should be drawn to the ecumenical importance of chapter six of the Schema, "The Place of Scripture in the Life of the Church." There are declarations here which unite Protestant and Catholic completely in our common attitude toward the Bible. Too often there have been objections from the Catholic side (against the Protestant theory) that the Bible is a dead letter and that only tradition is a living element. But in paragraph 24 of the Schema we read this wonderful sentence: "In the Holy Scriptures the Father who is in heaven meets His children with great love and speaks with them." Alongside the lacuna which I have noted from the Protestant perspective, there are many elements in this Schema which unite us, but the sentence I have just cited marks an area where accord is complete.

2. MARIOLOGY

If I have never concerned myself with the place which Mary occupies in Western Catholicism and in the Eastern Orthodox churches, it is because I have difficulties in finding a common base for dialogue on the subject. The problems which up to the present time have formed the object of my discussions with Catholic theologians are precisely those problems which we have in common—even if our solutions are different. But the cult of the saints and Mariology do not constitute valid theological problems for us. If we take as our point of departure the New Testament, we find only the problem of the fate of those who are "dead in Christ" before the end of time, which is to say before the resurrection of the body. For this reason, only this question interests me exegetically.[1]

As for the elements in the Roman Catholic doctrine and piety concerning Mary which are acceptable or unacceptable, I can accept the Catholics speaking of the election of Mary as "blessed among women," of her humility, of her faith, of her grief before the cross. But the Bible speaks of other men and women elected to be special instruments in salvation history. A man or woman who is elected is always chosen (and therefore "blessed") from among other men and women (Luke 1:42). In this respect is it legitimate to attribute to Mary a superiority of degree in her election over the other elected instruments of the divine plan, since she was elected to be the mother of the Son of God?

I cannot accept the manner in which Catholic exegesis minimizes the momentary absence of Mary's faith which is spoken of in Mark 3:21-33. In this passage the mother and brothers of Jesus wish to bring Him back home, saying of Him, "He is crazy." But Jesus, pointing to those who sat about Him listening, replies, "Here are my mother and brothers."

Neither can I accept the overly rapid exegesis which Catholics give to the question of Christ in John 2:4, "What have you to do with me?" Ought we not make an analogy between these episodes and the faltering of Peter's faith when he wants to keep Jesus from suffering (Mark 8:31ff., "Get thee behind me Satan!"), but who is later converted when he understands the redemptive significance of the death of Christ? Isn't the meaning of John 19:25ff. precisely this: at the cross of Christ Mary's faith was revived, and thus the cross created the true family of believers ("behold thy mother, behold thy son") of which Jesus speaks in Mark 3:33? The current Catholic exegesis of Rev. 12 also seems to be too superficial and too rapid (i.e., we have to take into account the eschatological Jewish texts, e.g., Qumran, also).

It seems certain to me that the recognition of Mary as an

---

[1] For Prof. Cullmann's stimulating discussion of this exegetical question, see *Immortality of the Soul or Resurrection of the Dead?*, London: Epworth, 1958.

elected instrument of God cannot justify a "Mariology" or a "Marian" cult. It is not possible to have a Mariology alongside a Christology any more than it is possible to have a "Petrology," in spite of the important place which Peter occupies in the history of salvation, or a "Paulology," or, if we go back to the Old Testament, an "Abrahamology," although Abraham is the exemplary instrument of divine election. There cannot be other "mediators," because the New Testament proclaims that there is "only one mediator, Jesus Christ." To affirm that the mediation of Mary is "included" in that of Christ is the same as saying that all men whom God has used to carry out His plan of salvation are themselves also mediators. The cult of the saints, moreover, is excluded by Rev. 19:10 and 22:8-9.

The dogmas of the Immaculate Conception and of the Bodily Assumption have no biblical foundation. On the contrary, they witness to a certain tendency which already appears in the *apocryphal* gospel accounts of the infancy (e.g., in the proto-gospel of James) which considers Mary no longer in *direct* dependence on Christ but makes her an independent object of veneration.[2]

I do not think that new events in the development of Mariology can be anticipated. The Conciliar discussion up to the present has proved rather that a majority of the fathers of the Council is committed to prevent all elaboration of Mariology and the cult of Mary. By demanding that Mary be spoken of only in the text "On the Church" and not, as the opposition would have desired, in an independent text, this majority has clearly demonstrated its intention to refrain from continuing to speak of Mary except in direct dependence on Christ. However, this majority cannot insist that the already existing dogmas be abolished. Rather, they wish to maintain Mariology and the cult of Mary as it is, and I am certain that they could not accept the point of view that I have offered here.

In spite of this, we ought to rejoice sincerely both in the attitude of these fathers and in the fact that they have commanded

[2] See Prof. Cullmann's article in Heenecke-Schneemelcher, *New Testament Apocrypha* (ET revised and edited by R. McL. Wilson) Phila., Westminster, 1963, "Infancy Gospels", pp. 370-388.

a majority vote. If the majority has been very small in this case, smaller than in the votes on other questions, this proves not only the immense pressure exerted within the Council, but also the fact that it is not only a theological problem but a devotional problem in which emotional elements play a significant role. This may be explained, it seems to me, by a monophysite theology in practice which has always characterized the popular piety of the Catholics. In spite of the Council of Chalcedon in which Christ was declared "fully God, fully man," the "fully man" is not taken with sufficient seriousness by Catholicism. The Son is thus confused with the Father in popular piety, ceasing to be the true mediator for men. From this arises the tendency to transfer to Mary the "humanity" of Christ. Popular piety feels itself closer to Mary than to Christ.

III

Have Expectations Been Fulfilled?

This chapter is a translation by James Hester of an address before the German Press Bureau on December 2, 1965, at the close of the Council. It was published originally in mimeographed form by the Centrum Coordinationis Communicationum de Concilio in Rome.

Not all of the address has been translated; in particular those things which are more highly developed in the long article "The Reform of Vatican II . . ." are left out. Those paragraphs which are translated were chosen for the additions they make to the more developed arguments of that article.

The two articles have in common Professor Cullmann's concern to show how wide an influence the concept aggiornamento *had at the Council and what concepts need to be added to that one in order for it to be legitimate. What this article adds to the longer one are his reflections on the side lights of the Council and his plea for a proper understanding of and application of ecumenism.*

HAVE EXPECTATIONS been fulfilled? Perhaps this question is premature, for Vatican Council II, in an even greater degree than earlier councils, can really be judged only together with its effects. Precisely because in many of the final texts two opposing theses, one old (Catholic syncretism)* and one new (biblical centrality), are placed together, it will only later be discernible whether or not the things which are significant now will be effectively fol-

---

* (Perhaps better: syncretistic tendency. Tr.)

lowed through in the future. At the convocation of the Council, John XXIII already indicated this when he declared that the Council pursued a long-range goal, in any case in ecumenical relations: later conversations with non-Catholic Christians, which must be conducted after the Council, should be eased by the altered viewpoint of the Catholic Church. But even the alterations within the church are so constituted that generally they could be effective only after the Council.

As always when I speak about the Council, I want explicitly to stress that I speak from the viewpoint of a Protestant observer,[1] and to be sure of a Protestant observer who at no time forgets that our Protestant churches also constantly require renewal. We all have need of constant change (*Umkehr*). Our question should really run, "Have our Protestant expectations been fulfilled?" And I should add yet another limitation; although I am at one with my fellow believers, each one can really speak only of his own expectations. Consequently each one must take into account the other's unavoidable subjectiveness which affects any judgment of this Council.

Therefore I want to ask, what have we expected of the Council as such? Here we must first of all differentiate between legitimate expectations and illusions, for unjustified expectations could not be fulfilled *a priori*. Three years ago I spoke in the Press Bureau at the beginning of the first session. Among other things I tried to mention those things which we could *not* expect. At that time that was necessary, for it was a time of enthusiasm, of euphoria, which ruled both Catholics and Protestants. But particularly there were also illusions. At that time I had to warn above all my fellow believers about these things. It was the time when we had to react against naïve remarks such as those which we often heard in meetings with lay persons and read in letters from lay circles, "hopefully you [that is, Protestants and Catholics] will come to terms at the Council." As if this Council could be considered as a council for unity! At every ecumenical gathering I had warned again and again even before the Council of the

[1] See "The Role of the Observers at the Vatican Council" for a fuller, somewhat differently oriented, discussion, pp. 102-106.

danger of overlooking those things which stand in the way of complete agreement between Catholics and Protestants, of overlooking the limits of approximation: to believe that there could be fusion, or to assume that the Catholic Church could give up earlier dogmas, e.g., the primacy of the pope. Those who overlooked these limits could only experience disappointment, a disappointment which must produce a crippling effect on the ecumenical endeavor. For it has actually come about that precisely the ones who at that time had high-flying, fully unfounded hopes today declare their distinterest in the Council. They blame the unfulfillment of their illusions to the change of popes, as if John XXIII would and could have fulfilled every figment of their imaginations. Now they agree with the blasé and self-righteous remarks of those who had said from the beginning that nothing would come from the Council and that the Catholic Church will not change. At that time we had also to fight this position, for we had expected some alteration by this Council from the beginning.

What did we expect? Only the definition of the goal which Pope John XXIII gave in his opening speech could be the correct basis for legitimate expectations. One must always start with it: "The authentic teaching of the church should be studied and described according to the methods of research and the forms of expression which modern thinking uses. The substance of the old teaching which is contained in the deposit of faith is to be distinguished from the formulation in which it is dressed." Then John made it clear that this formulation should take into consideration pastoral and ecumenical aspects. Negatively he decided that no heresies should be condemned, no new dogmas formulated, and no old dogmas repeated, "tasks which do not require a council."

One expectation is tied up with what John XXIII said in his definition of substance and formulation. (Since the word "substance" has become somewhat disreputable, I want to replace it here with the word "kernel" [*Kern*] which is not philosophically or theologically encumbered.) So it is a question of the relationship between the center of Catholic teaching and the formulation in which it is dressed, in other words, it is a question of the oft-mentioned *aggiornamento,* which can be translated "modernization" or "adaptation."[2] In fact our expectations are *also* related to that. Many times before the Council we had spoken in two different languages, and this has extraordinarily impeded mutual understanding. On the one hand, the Protestant formulation since the sixteenth century has oriented itself to biblical forms of expression. At the same time it has thoroughly accommodated itself in the following centuries to the speech of the modern world. On the other hand, the Catholic formulation has remained thoroughly scholastic.

However, I wish to stress with special emphasis that renewal of the *Christian Church* may not be a merely a question of adaptation to the modern world. *Aggiornamento* may never be an *isolated motive* for renewal. John XXIII also perceived that when he spoke of the distinction between immutable substance and formulation. However, the question concerning the border between invariable substance and formulation presents a highly difficult and complex problem. This problem has not been dealt with by either John or the Council. Perhaps it could not be in this framework. The Council appears to me to suffer at this point, because it regards the question concerning the border between the immutable substance and the formulation which is in need of alteration as already solved. (By no means do I thereby overlook the fact that many Protestant theologians also do not generally take notice of this question in their endeavor to make the biblical message accessible to the modern world. They too are guilty of syncretism.) The address of Paul VI on November 18, 1965, to be sure correctly endeavors to oppose a false conception of *aggiornamento.* Nevertheless he also was unable to clarify the matter. It must be admitted that the meaning of *aggiornamento* all by itself is not enough. It is quite useless to say that kernel and formulation must be distinguished, if it is not shown what kernel and formulation are.

But the problem lies deeper. Not only must the question con-

2 See section three of "The Reform . . .", pp. 76-77, 87-96, for a fuller discussion.

cerning the border be recognized, but also above all the new formulation may not be only an external concern, but must have its foundation in the kernel itself. The reason the Protestant Reformation was able to call forth so great an effect was because its basic principle was not the abolition of contemporary grievances, as it is often described, not *aggiornamento*. Its opposition to grievances proceeded primarily from a theme of faith. Thus *aggiornamento* should be only an emanation of an impulse which comes out of the kernel; *aggiornamento* should be a consequence, not a starting point.

The enthusiasm of the first session has disappeared, but this has been the case with every reform movement, even in the Reformation of the sixteenth century. Nevertheless, we have been able to ascertain that there has been an intensification in the subsequent sessions without this enthusiasm. All too quickly we forget that much which appeared revolutionary and was hotly disputed in the first session became commonplace by the second session. Also the will for renewal was at work in the reaction against certain regrettable incidents. But above all, it can not be forgotten that all the voting shows that a significant majority of the Council fathers desired renewal from the beginning to the end of the Council. To be sure, we had hoped for this before the Council began, but we were not at all sure that we could expect it. The existence of this majority at the Council must always be remembered. The interventions of the Council fathers are witness to this desire for renewal even more than the texts. If anywhere, we perceive something of the spirit of Pentecost about which John XXIII had spoken precisely in many of these short testimonies, which often seemed to us to be prophetic preaching in the best sense. They richly compensated for the other interventions and also repetitions which many times allowed our interest to flag.

Things which have taken place at the Council have exceeded our expectations more than the texts. We had never reckoned that we would be treated with so much respect, confidence, and tact at the Council by the Secretariat for Promoting Christian

Unity presided over by Cardinal Bea when we received the invitation from them to be an observer.[3] The place under the Longinus statue, where we obviously had an excellent vantage point, may be a continuing historical witness not only to the fact that non-Catholic observers could not take part in a Council of the Catholic Church, but also to the extensive confidence with which we became initiated without mental reservations into all secrets and received all texts to read in their original form. Only in this way could we generally determine such things as precisely that much discussed alteration in the Schema on Ecumenism concerning the words "find" and "seek" God, which distressed us merely by the fact that the alteration had occurred.[4] I wish, nevertheless, to confirm even in this painful matter this positive thing, the confidence and openness which was offered us. Also far exceeding our expectations was the character which our discussions assumed in the Secretariat concerning the items which were dealt with by the Council, the frankness with which we were able to express openly our opinions there, and the hearing which was given to us by those in the highest positions. We will not forget the Tuesday afternoons, first in the Hotel Columbus and later in the hospitable Foyer Unitas, with Msgr. Willebrands at the Praesidium. And we had not foreseen all of our many other delightful and fruitful contacts in the passageways or at the famous "bars" in the Church of St. Peter or by invitation to meals by cardinals, bishops, and periti.

Finally I come to that which concerns us Protestants the most: the ecumenism of the post-Council times. There is today a fashionable ecumenism which seems to me to endanger the thing to which we want to be of service. Ecumenism has become a slogan. There is frankly an *ecumenical jubilation,* which, like all ecclesiastical jubilation, is not a good thing. It overlooks the limits which are placed on the Church: it disregards that which I call the tension between the already completed "now" (*schon*) and the yet outstanding "not yet" (*noch nicht*).[5] Earlier, yet not so long

3 See "The Role . . .", pp. 103-104.
4 For a fuller discussion, see "The Reform . . .", p. 86.
5 See "The Theology . . .", pp. 41 ff.

ago, it took courage to engage in ecumenical conversations, and especially to carry out ecumenical acts. Today ecumenism has almost become a means by which to become famous. As much as this development is in itself to be greeted, there seems to me to be a great danger included in it. Ecumenism may not become either a *fashion* or even less an *institution*.

Ecumenical sentimentalism is also a danger. Because in the context of this Council we have come so extraordinarily close, we risk on all sides rendering the remaining divergences harmless. We thereby only endanger the business of seeking a wider area of agreement, a broader approximation. I have in mind here precisely the relationship with our Catholic friends to whom we stand theologically closest by nature. At the Council we have largely shared their expectations, cares, and joys, even their disappointments. And as I ask my question concerning the fulfillment of expectations, it would also in large part be the expectations of our close Catholic friends. Nevertheless, it would be dangerous to be of the opinion that unity with us might be realized if that faction of the Catholic Church ultimately succeeded. I want to give warning in the face of this illusion precisely in the interest of future dialogue. Certainly the conversations have been facilitated by the results which were reached by our friends at the Council. We are sincerely pleased by that. But we would destroy the fruits of the Council if we would now pass over in silence the things which further separate us.

I am thinking about Schemata like the one concerning revelation.[6] What separates us here in spite of all the satisfactory things is not perhaps the things which were added in the last hours, but that which grows out of the Protestant position of Scripture as a norm for the tradition of the Church. At this point not even our friends could be in agreement with us, and we not with them. Concerning this, as also with many other questions, the future dialogue has to be conducted, but with all uninhibited openness.

All too often in the past years I have experienced ecumenical conversations where the Catholic partner has merely stressed how

6 See "Two Interviews . . .", pp. 46-50.

near Catholic teaching is to Protestant, and vice versa. True, we should be pleased about the things we have in common. We should learn from one another. We should not, however, pass over divergences in silence but speak with one another precisely about *them*.

A further danger, which is especially acute on both sides today, exists also in the dialogue about controversial questions themselves: namely, that divergences will be gone into but then all too quickly explained away. Certainly dialogue should bring us closer together, but the things that still separate us should be recognized with all clarity and not rendered harmless by what are often artificial interpretations, so that the resultant discussions dispense with clarity. Dialogue should be conducted in full clarity and truth, not in confusion. If there is *then* an approximation of viewpoints, this is immensely more valuable. But also if it must be provisionally determined at the end of the conversation that the two positions are incompatible at the point under discussion, it is ecumenically much better than if one separated in an illusionary unity. Thus I want to confess that I rather welcomed some of the additions to the Council outlines. I welcomed them because those things which separate us had been implicitly present in the texts anyhow, and now they were spelled out clearly. On the other hand, there were naturally cases of additions which brought in a new thought that was not in the text and was even in opposition to the thought of the text.

Today the danger exists that those Protestants and Catholics who go as far as possible in suppressing and rendering harmless real divergences will be labeled "ecumenically progressive." I think that this error should be removed. Certainly I do not want, thereby, to recommend as good ecumenists those who with the same onesidedness on the other side systematically see only the things which separate us. They know that I reject this radical position also.

When we go home, we will have to battle, especially in lay circles, both the false ecumenical sentimentality and the opposition in principle against proximity. It will be one of the great tasks of the post-Council times to bring to the laity the true ecumenical position for church people which was so satisfactorily strengthened by the theologians of the Council. Here much is given to do, and the fulfillment of the Council expectations in ecumenical relations is dependent upon it. Our thinking and conversations in our ecumenical institutes are too exclusively on the level of theologians for the times following the Council. The Decree on Ecumenism mentions some of the means which are suited to promote ecumenism *among the laity*. May I say that I personally consider it one of my unfulfilled expectations that the Council did not include one of means which is biblically anchored and goes back to the early church, to the Apostles' Council, namely, that of a yearly reciprocal collection.[7] Nevertheless, it had been mentioned in the Council by Cardinal Silva Henriquez, the president of the Caritas and the Bishop of Arras. I am convinced that precisely this means, which is already widely practiced, will bring among the laity the ecumenical spirit. Precisely because I advocate an absolute realism and see the difficulties of a final theological alliance, I welcome everything that presently makes visible on a practical level the unity which *already* exists in Christ. To that end I count first of all mutual prayer. Therefore, I consider the initiative of the Pope in celebrating in the Basilica of San Paolo—the selection of the place is of highest significance—a common farewell worship service with the Protestant observers, with Bible reading and prayer as one of the most important ecumenical acts of the Council. Certainly it will bear fruit which will be much more meaningful for the ecumenical cause than much theological dispute.

If at the close of the Council I say in *retrospect* that on the whole the expectations, insofar as they were not illusions, and apart from individual instances, have been fulfilled and in many cases exceeded; and if I express the conviction in *anticipation* of action in the future that the Catholic Church will further change its view within the limits of continuity and that our approximation will make further progress, I do so because I am convinced that alongside all other spirits, in spite of diplomacy and agitation, *the Holy Spirit was also at work*. He was at work when

7 Cp. *Message to Catholics and Protestants*, Grand Rapids: Eerdmans, 1959.

this Council was called together, conducted, and brought to a close. There are always setbacks, and there have been setbacks in salvation history from the first. It is not superficial optimism if at the end of the Council I contradict those who say, "Nothing in the Catholic Church will change after this Council; everything will go on as it did before the Council." That which might be designated as optimism is in reality taking the third article of our common confession of faith in earnest: "I believe in the Holy Spirit." I am also convinced that salvation history continues, though not in everything which happens in the Church and certainly not in everything which has happened and which was fixed at this Council. Recognizing that it is always risky to declare something is the mysterious work of God in the present, I want, however, to explain this Council in the light of the revelation given to us in Jesus Christ and under the preservation of all dimensions which are thereby given; on the whole I look at this Council as an element of salvation history.

"Do not quench the Holy Spirit," admonishes the apostle Paul. The Holy Spirit presupposes constant *readiness for repentance*. If renewal shall move forward through the Spirit, the Church must always be ready for renewal, and I might add: all churches, even ours. This conviction stands behind my entire report, behind my critical remarks also. For we must all be constantly renewed by the Holy Spirit. Only thus will our expectations for the entire Church of Christ be fulfilled.

IV

The Reform of Vatican Council II
in the Light of the History of
the Catholic Church

This chapter is the apex of this volume. It was written some time after the close of the Council, at a time after Professor Cullmann was able to consider the whole Council in his reflections. It was used in translation as a series of lectures when Professor Cullmann was in the United States in the fall of 1966, and has appeared in Theologische Literaturzeitung *(Jan. '67). Here Professor Cullmann draws together and more fully develops many of the insights represented in the shorter chapters. This is his most recent thinking.*

The central thesis of this chapter is that there truly has been a reform of the Catholic Church at the Council. The reform is not simply modernization of external forms but a new appreciation for the Bible. However, this reform has not been, indeed could not be, carried out with all its ramifications. The entire chapter aims at demonstrating this thesis and closes by pointing out what this means for Protestant-Catholic dialogue. The chapter was translated by James Hester.

IT IS TOO EARLY to align Vatican Council II in church history in the same way that we, as historians, could place the earlier councils in relation to the broad development of Catholicism throughout the centuries. To draw a final historical assessment in this sense would be premature, as if this Council, more than the past ones, had a long-range goal in view. We must recognize this barrier if we try in the following pages the all too bold attempt to

determine the place of the most recent Council in church history.

It is unnecessary to analyze all the texts of the Council here. This has been done enough already. The already comprehensive literature of the Council will grow from day to day. The texts are now available in good manageable editions in Latin and in translation. It will certainly be a while yet until the Vatican will have published the collected Acts, the first as well as the subsequent drafts which were progressively altered, and above all the interventions of the Council fathers. But also different from the time of the earlier councils is the fact that this time, especially since the second session, the essential points of these preliminary stages were already published during the deliberations by the daily press. This time in many cases the "secret character of the Council" was only a fiction. Meanwhile, the developments which have led to the final texts have been repeatedly described in context. We will, therefore, speak only of the Council within the framework of our topic.

However, it is important for a historically correct assessment of the Council to draw conclusions not only from the collection of texts. The danger of that kind of unhistorical methodology will become even greater the further we move away in time from the Council. It is more important for this Council than for any earlier Council to consider not only the texts but also the events of the Council, the things that took place there. For already, according to the first declarations of John XXIII, the texts proclaimed by Vatican II should be worked out as guidelines rather than as dogmatic proclamations. *Vaticanum secundum* is an "impulse" rather than a "text." It does not discuss a number of definite problems as the earlier councils did, but rather the entire teaching and entire life of the church. Thus not only the *sub secreto* drafts which were printed and handed to the Council fathers and observers must be considered alongside the final texts, but also the discussions about them.

In all councils there has been conflict among different parties. With regard to the character of the Council of 1962-65, which was mentioned above, the recognition of this altercation with all the secondary aspects is even more important than before. For in order to judge whether or not the reforms which are defined in the texts are really reforms, their inspiration must be known, and the often directly prophetical interventions of the bishops and cardinals in the Basilica of St. Peter which were the stimulating elements of the Council must be recognized. Further, the heated discussions in the Commissions, which continued in the passageways of the Basilica, must be known, and certainly the machinations, intrigues, and diplomatic actions which are always present at council meetings must be recognized.

It should be asked—not without apprehension—whether for the future the impulse which had motivated the original form of the texts will still be generally discernible and evident for later generations; for this impulse, even though it shows through for those who took part in the Council, has been progessively weakened in the altered drafts of most constitutions and decrees. Here we can only hope and trust that the will for renewal which came so powerfully to expression in all those oral Conciliar interventions, but also in the strong reaction against hindering influences, will not be suppressed even more, although many texts contain only a weak echo of the original impulse.

In any case it is also important in this regard that not only the texts but also the events of the Council be portrayed, and fortunately we can see in the overwhelming wave of literature on the Council that in some books at least something of the atmosphere in which the texts arose is being preserved in personal memories, in anecdotes, and even in the witticisms of the Council.

The prophetic earnestness for the success of the reform which John XXIII and the majority of the Council wished may never be lost from view as the starting point of the consideration of the texts.

Reform in the Christian Church means two things: on the one hand, it is the development of a genuine Christian principle which has been suppressed or pushed into the background in the passing of the centuries and hindered in its development. On the other hand, it is the elimination of distortions. Both kinds of reform presuppose concentration on the kernel of the Christian message. This kernel must be both the standard of the development and the criteria of the elimination of illegitimate elements. We will investigate if and how far Vatican Council II in this sense has realized a reform, seen in the light of church history.

The question whether or not reform has been realized is today often answered in the negative from the Protestant side. Many Protestants say, when the texts are read carefully and all restrictions taken into precise consideration, that it could be decided in the final analysis that "nothing has changed," and that once again it has turned out to be true that Catholicism is not capable of reform from the ground up. On the other hand, one hears from both enthusiastic Protestants and Catholics that Catholicism has radically altered itself. In the illusionary expectation of a speedy and complete reunification they see in the reforms which materialized from the Council a suppression, an elmination of all those things which fundamentally separated us, as if now only secondary problems stood in the way of a complete fusion.

Both judgments—"nothing changed," "everything changed"— are false. They rest on false presuppositions and illusions, not the least of which is the refusal to see the inevitable limits of a Catholic reform. Therefore, we will speak of these limits.

1. THE LIMITS OF EVERY CATHOLIC RENEWAL AND THE POSSIBILITIES
OF REFORM WHICH ARE REALIZED WITHIN THIS FRAMEWORK OF THE
COUNCIL

Protestant disappointments in Catholicism, "which never changes," are many times the result of false expectations, like the ones which could be encountered immediately before the opening of the Council even in lay circles. From the outset it should be clear that there is a limit set to every Catholic renewal which was not there for the Protestant Reformation and does not exist for any further Protestant renewal. In spite of all linking of the Reformers to the ancient Christian symbols, the Bible is the only standard for a Protestant renewal. For Catholicism the dogmas of the Church and its living tradition, in which it sees a development of the Bible, are also essential. As soon as it would give up this fundamental attitude and thus place its very base, its foundation, in question, it would cease to be Catholicism, for it would already stand in a place contrary to its own fundamentals.

Vatican Council II would and could be only a Catholic council. Disregard of this fact has led to the playing off of the two popes of the Council, John XXIII and Paul VI, against one another. With all the fundamental differences of their personalities which have operated in the leading of the Council, John XXIII, to whom today has been incorrectly assigned a radicalism, something foreign to him, desired a *Catholic renewal* in a *Catholic framework*.

That means, therefore, that it could not be the goal of the Council to change as such something in the wording of the early dogmas. Strictly speaking, the obvious knowledge of this fact should show the limit which is set for every Catholic reform, in contrast to Protestant reforms. In as much as the socalled Catholic modernism which was condemned at the beginning of the century wanted to include the same dogmas in the process of modernization, it necessarily had to fail.

Now, however, the significant thing at this Council is exactly that it has succeeded to renew Catholicism, as has hardly ever been the case in its long history; it has even succeeded in moderating the rigidity of the dogmas without altering the smallest things in the wording. This has become possible in two ways. On the one hand, an opposite thesis, so to say, in which the will for renewal comes to expression has been placed alongside the unaltered text of the old dogma. On the other hand, a *shifting* inside of the kernel of the established Catholic teaching which is established by the dogma is undertaken due to the principle of renewal in such a way that an order of preference is set forth among the truths which are expressed in the dogmas, and greater meaning is assigned to one than to another.

It must be recognized for the future of the promising possibilities of reform that both methods are, nevertheless, accomplished within the limits of the unalterable character of the existing dogma. Concerning the first of these methods—consisting in the juxtaposition of the old dogma and a kind of antithesis

—this very clever method has become a source of reproach to the Council. Only deceit and insincere diplomacy could be seen here, because the limits of Catholicism, which cannot be transgressed, have not been observed by those who want Roman Catholicism to remain Roman Catholicism.

Indeed we see almost everywhere in most texts that generally where bold new declarations are made which have been inspired mostly by the Bible, the dogmas which often represent the opposite tendency are simultaneously stressed with special force.

This juxtaposition appears in two basic and especially important texts: in the Constitution "De Revelatione" and in "De Ecclesia." The final text of "De Revelatione" (also called "Dei Verbum" after the first words) has been correctly designated one of the most satisfying declarations of this Council. Previously a completely backward and negative text concerning the (two) "sources of revelation" had arisen for discussion in the first session. Fortunately it was rejected. Now only *one* revelation is admitted in the final text, and the text contains, as we shall see, astoundingly positive statements about the central role of the Bible and about Bible study as the "soul of theology." Enthusiastic Protestants and Catholics, who seem to me thereby to endanger the ecumenical cause, have declared after the proclamation of this Constitution that now no longer does a fundamental difference stand between Catholics and Protestants in this controversial question about Scripture and tradition. Closer investigation of the texts, nevertheless, shows that in spite of these positive declarations the traditional distinction between Scripture and tradition is not fundamentally altered. For the equivalent position of these two elements has only shifted in the final text: the origin is indeed now a unique revelation, but there is a transmission which, as always, proceeds on two equally important ways, Scripture and tradition. The two stand in close association with one another, and it is said concerning them, "Both Scripture and tradition are to be received with equal reverence and held in equal esteem." Here we cannot agree.

Thus we remain separated, now as before, in the definition of the mutual relationship of Scripture and tradition and the teaching office. Tradition and the teaching office are expressly placed here on the same level with one another, *inter se connectuntur,* closely connected. In reality the Protestant church also stresses that Scripture is exegeted *within* the Church (but not *by* the Church). True, the New Testament books have originated in the early church, which does continue in our congregations. We also admit in principle the necessity of a teaching office (certainly not infallible, since a further source of error is thereby created). Church tradition can help to unlock the positive blessings of the Bible which have unfolded in the passing of the centuries. However, there are in the Church not only legitimate but also illegitimate traditions, not only development but also distortion. On these grounds it is not enough according to the Protestant teaching to compare the three great elements as intimately connected to one another, and to permit Scripture to be interpreted only by the Church. Scripture fulfills not only a positive role of mediating revelation but also has to exercise a judicial function in order to differentiate in the postapostolic tradition (for the apostles the problem proved to be something different)[1] legitimate development from distortion. As soon as Scripture has to fulfill this judicial function, it cannot be interpreted by the Church as such. Otherwise the Church would be its own judge. Rather there must be a confrontation between the Bible and the Church. The Bible must address the Church. It must be the critical standard, a superior court over the Church. Unfortunately the word "norm" which stands in an earlier draft has disappeared from the final text.

Thus things which had been expressly condemned by the Reformers stand in these sentences of the same Constitution which is exceedingly welcome in other connections, "The Church draws her certainty . . . not only from Scripture." In an almost monotonous manner the tradition is added to the significant role of Scripture. On that point there was exaggerated excitement, shortly before the proclamation of this Constitution, that such additions had been made. The fact that the Bible has not been

1 See my article in *The Early Church* (London, 1956), "The Tradition: The Exegetical, Historical and Theological Problem," pp. 55-99.

placed as a higher standard above tradition and the teaching office was certain anyhow if one considers carefully the entire text. It is far better for the clarity of the discussion that there be no possible doubt about that. According to the texts of the Council, tradition and the teaching office are not dethroned by Scripture, but on the contrary, the old teaching as it was defined at Trent retains its value.

We have begun with the example of the Constitution "De Revelatione" because it properly demonstrates the *limits* of reform which are set on all other decisions of the Council in teaching and life. Here we can ascertain in principle that the Bible is given throughout the text a significance which it has never before possessed in the Catholic Church. However, it is still not granted the *exclusive* position which it must properly demand out of its innermost essence. Furthermore, in the future the Catholics will continue to say, Bible *and* tradition, Bible *and* teaching office. They must say that, for otherwise the foundation of the Catholic Church would be lost.

Are they who maintain that nothing has changed correct? Yes and no. They are correct insofar as it becomes evident exactly from the declaration of this Constitution that even the boldest desire for reform which is inspired by the Bible is always bound by the old restrictive dogmas so that everything seemingly remains with the old. And nevertheless they are incorrect, for the old dogmas are weakened, in spite of everything, by the resultant connection with the vigorous new declaration concerning the individuality of the Bible. We may even hope that the Bible will be made more and more effective by its indwelling power in all spheres and by its claim to primacy in spite of theories which run otherwise.

Is it justified to reproach the Council and above all the Pope, Paul VI, with ambivalence because he often—albeit under the pressure of the conservative minority—intervened directly in the juxtaposition of the old dogma with the new thesis? When we remember that every Catholic reform that really wants to be a *Catholic* reform has the above-mentioned limit set, then it must on the contrary be recognized as progress, historically speaking,

that the Council has adopted this new way in the history of
Catholic theology to weaken the dogmas, even though we might
as Protestants deplore the fact that the thesis inspired from the
Bible alone could not succeed.

It might be insisted that this is not so new. Catholicism might
always be characterized as "a mixture of opposites." This may
be affirmed, but the endeavor to assimilate opposites has not had
as a goal in the past a *reduction* of the scope of the old dogmas.
This is what characterizes the Council, i.e., connecting those
things which are opposites.

We could determine in almost all the collected texts of Vatican
Council II this coexistence of two theses which simultaneously
points out the limit of all Catholic reform and the possibilities
of accomplishing real reform in spite of those limits. I need only
cite "De Ecclesia." In this Constitution, this kind of renewal within
the old framework is especially evident in the question of the
relation between the dogma on the primacy of the Pope as it
has been described in 1870, and the new, now resultant, proclamation of the collegiality of the bishops. The latter represents an
important renewal by Vatican II. Insofar as it allows the bishops
great rights and a certain joint-ruling with the Pope, the structure of the Catholic Church in this way certainly comes nearer
that of the Church of the New Testament. The old controversy
which was settled in the earlier reform councils about the "episcopacy" and "curiality" has experienced an orientation in the
direction of the episcopacy because of this strong emphasis on
"collegiality." And yet we state the same thing again: the old
dogma of 1870, in this case that of the primacy of the Pope who
can make decisions on his own, has not been overturned, for it
could not be overturned.

The entire text concerning this collegiality implicitly mentions
this fact. Thus the paradoxical situation has resulted that the
dogma of primacy is mentioned in this section more often than
in the texts of the Council of 1870! In somewhat almost comical
ways every statement concerning the collegiality of the bishops
is expanded by the indication that the primacy of the Pope is
not hurt by collegiality. Some Council theologians have even

counted how many times the primacy of the Pope is stressed in a few pages, where otherwise the dogma of 1870 should have been essentially weakened.

It can only be a question of a juxtaposition of both theses, not of an essential synthesis, for otherwise the dogma of 1870 would have to be considered anew and would have to be modified, something which is not possible in Catholicism. That is especially clear in the exegesis clause for the text concerning the collegiality of the bishops which was announced in the third session. In this clause it is said, on the one hand, that the authority of the Church is exercised by the bishops when they concur in a decision with the Pope. However, on the other hand, the Pope can make decisions alone. The friends of reform have been exceedingly irritated by that clause. I believe that here also it was good for the sake of clarity that what already stood more or less hidden in the text was now said openly.

Therefore, even here the old continues although a change has begun. Thus in fact not only did Paul VI intervene decisively at the end of the third session. John XXIII had already intervened twice in the first session (with the admitting of Joseph into the canon of the Mass, and, corresponding to be sure with the will of the majority but also contradictory to the Constitution of the Council, with the rejection of the old-fashioned first draft on "the two sources of revelation").

The same unavoidable ambivalence which is the consequence of the limits of any Catholic reform shows up in the practical establishment of a synod of bishops in the fourth session. It is important as an advisory council, and yet it is dependent on the Pope to be convened. A real synthesis is and remains excluded here. The dogma of primacy belongs essentially to the structure of the Catholic Church, and yet moderation of the dogma has come because of the addition of collegiality. Progressive popes who will be inclined to go further along this way could depend upon these new texts and new institutions. On the other hand, it also remains true that future popes in whom this desire will not be present, as it was and is present with the two popes of the Council, could hold to the old dogma alone. In any case we should recognize that the only way of minimizing the dogma has been used and precisely with this goal in mind.

In the same Constitution concerning the Church we are able to make a similar observation in the last chapter, the one which deals with Mary. Here also an evident moderation of the dogma on Mary is sought. But here again the desire for renewal has not been able to operate to the end. Certainly abuse of the popular Mary piety is fortunately warned against in that last chapter. Also the inclusion of the text on Mary in the last chapter of "De Ecclesia" (after many passionate discussions) was considered generally to be a minimizing of Mariology over against the original intention to devote a special independent Schema to her—such a one was already printed. Perhaps, nevertheless, the present order of the text can also operate as a strengthening of Mariology. It now appears as the apex of all the statements about the Church. In an effort to weaken Mariology it is stressed that all honor of Mary belongs in the final analysis to Christ. But the irrevocable dogmas of Mary retain their full importance, and among the many titles of honor—even though imbedded in many others—she is nevertheless now called that which is biblically objectionable, the Mediatrix.

Here the practical veneration which belongs to the heart of Catholic piety has to be taken into account apart from the dogma, and with it the emotional elements which are thereby produced.[2] Therefore, the essential moderation which is aimed for in the other texts through the coexistence of statements has not occurred in Mariology. It is really the only point where it must be said that even a certain hardening by the Council has taken place. This statement obtains its validity less from the text mentioned above than from all the things which happened at the Council: papal addresses to the Council, appointment of the beginning and end of the Council on festival days for Mary, proclamation of Mary as "Mother of the Church," building of a new church in Rome which is dedicated to her, and so forth. That this effective strengthening was possible, in spite of the chapter which aimed at a weakening of Mariology, shows that also in this text two

2 See "Two Interviews . . .", esp. the last answer concerning Mariology.

tendencies have come to expression and that as soon as the conservative tendency complied with the will of the Pope or the majority, the conservative statements could win the upper hand in the practical application, even if in its original intention the text aimed at a kind of moderation. Nevertheless, this desire for reform may succeed in the majority of the other cases.

We have mentioned before, along with the possibility of a minimizing or weakening of the old dogma by the addition of a contrasting thesis, an entirely different way that has exceedingly great potential, which likewise realizes the intention of reform without changing the wording of the text as such: the *shifting* which is undertaken among the different dogmas making up the center of Catholic teaching. Out of the principle of renewal certain dogmatic statements are stressed more strongly, others less strongly, than before. Also by these expedients the limit which is fixed for Catholic reform by dogmas and tradition is not removed, but a wider latitude inside this limit is furnished for the desire for renewal. The various placing of emphases on the different dogmas permits, seen on the whole, an essential new orientation of the entire teaching of the Church.

Certainly in this preliminary statement only the principle has been articulated rather than all the consequences already drawn out of it. But for the future of the renewal this statement of the Council is one of the most helpful of all Council texts, even though, strange to say, so little has been said of it. It stands in the Decree "De Oecumenismo" (§11). Here it is explicitly said that there is an order of preference, a *hierarchy among the truths* of Catholic teaching, according to their relation to the fundamentals of the Catholic faith. Even though this is said at first only in view of the dialogue with the separated brethren, the entire Catholic teaching is affected by this principle independent of this dialogue. There may be similar statements here and there in earlier Catholic teaching. However, never before has this been expressed in an important Council text. Indeed there can be found up to the time of Pius XII texts which express the opposite, that all dogmas have the same value. According to this new text, naturally without this consequence already being drawn out, a lesser importance could be ascribed to the dogma concerning the assumption of Mary and to that of the primacy of the Pope than to the christological dogmas of the fourth and fifth centuries. From here immeasurable possibilities for the future move into view, especially those which concern the conversations between Catholics and Protestants. And further, it is significant that thereby the wording of the dogma as such will be completely preserved.

What appears to be the weakness of the Council to many, and above all naturally to us Protestants, namely that the dogmatic foundations with all their restrictive influences have remained the same and yet something new has become possible, may therefore actually amount to its strength when we consider that we are dealing with a Catholic council.

If this new thing would exist only in individual reforms which had not carried a common principle of renewal, then the prospect would be limited that the desire for renewal will operate in the future within the scope of the present limits. Precisely the preference for certain truths before others which was mentioned before presupposes one such unifying principle. This leads us to the second question.

2. DID THE COUNCIL STAND UNDER A UNIFYING PRINCIPLE OF RENEWAL?

We are inclined to answer this question *a priori* in the affirmative when we consider that John XXIII placed the Council under the watchword *aggiornamento,* which we could translate "adaptation" or "modernization."[3] This key word, which is certainly meant theologically in this connection, has then all too quickly become a slogan which departs from any theological content. Had *aggiornamento,* in the idea of a mere modernization of the Church and its teaching at any price and without regard for its center, actually been the only and essential principle of renewal, this Council would not have been inspired by the impulse which dwelt in it from the beginning and showed itself in the first

3 See "Have Expectations . . .", pp. 57-58.

session in a certain enthusiasm which is inherent in all reform movements in the first stages. Later this enthusiasm sometimes threatened to be overcome by a Council weariness. However, in a more moderate form it always remained at hand, and it even shines through all the compromises in the final texts. It should also be traceable in the future, in spite of that unavoidable ambivalence. Thus it continues its work. The slogan of modernization would have brought forth at the very most a passing flash of enthusiasm but no real intention of reform grounded in faith. What the Protestant renewal in the sixteenth century made into a real reformation was a theme of faith, not merely an external adaptation in the sense of an abolition of a few abuses.

Certainly it must be said that for a number of Council participants, the Council was nothing more than that which is meant by *aggiornamento* as a mere slogan. But in reality there was something much deeper at work in the texts as well as in the things which happened at the Council than a mere wish "to adapt" to the world. Otherwise we could not on the whole speak of reform. For we have seen that reform is both renewal by further development of neglected legitimate Christian tendencies *and* elimination of distortions or errors in development. Now the distortion in Catholicism, however, originates from an *aggiornamento* in former times which went too far; the danger of syncretism had not always been avoided. From the beginning of this Council, however, the desire for renewal by purification was resisted by elements which were added later and which counteracted the legitimate center of the gospel. In this respect, therefore, adaptation could not lead to purification.

Both methods of reform require a return behind the distortion to manifestations of legitimate ecclesiastical development in the past centuries. This endeavor leads instinctively, if it is consistently pursued, back to the *biblical beginnings of the Church*. What theoretically is not possible, because of the dogmatically established definition of the relation between Scripture and tradition, has come true in practice at least to a certain extent— certainly always within the established limits. The Bible has, in the last analysis, in many cases awakened both the critiques of traditional institutions and the wish to modify the rigidity of the existent dogmas.

In the course of the centuries the Bible and biblical thought had been suppressed by a purely speculative methodology which neglected the concrete historical action of God in history as it has been revealed to us in history. When that happens, the basis, the foundation, has been lost. Therefore, we must evaluate it positively if we now see in the decisive Council texts that the static-scholastic concepts have been replaced by biblical concepts of salvation history. We will see that precisely in this way only will theology become relevant for today, because it thus aligns the present into the living stream of past events. Thus *aggiornamento* is submitted to a theological principle and draws its content from it. This dynamic *biblical-historical* thinking has not yet entirely replaced the static conceptual thinking, but it has done so in decisive places, and in that I see the proper *theological theme* of the renewal by this Council.

Unfortunately, this biblical impulse has never been directly set up from the official Catholic side as the chief concept, and it is regrettable that instead of this, the slogan *aggiornamento* was the catchword. A certain fear of coming all too close to the Protestant Reformation by stressing the biblical principle might be to blame here. Nevertheless, the essential thing is that this theme was effective in consciously impressing the reform thought of the Council fathers. Pope John XXIII had named "ecumenical" and "pastoral" as the guiding principles of the Council. But these are only the consequences of the biblical theme.

The biblical renewal in Catholicism certainly began before the Council. Without this renewal, which we exegetes have seen for some twenty or thirty years, this Council would not be conceivable. The intensification of Bible study was precipitated by the encyclical concerning the study of the Bible which was announced by Pope XII more than twenty years ago. "Divino Afflante Spiritu." Its proclamation is one of the positive aspects of the disputed pontificate of Pius XII. Cardinal Bea, one-time rector of the Pontifical Biblical Institute, was greatly involved in its composition.

Before we show how in almost all decisive Council texts the biblical ferment (and thereby the ecumenical ferment which results from it) attempts to operate, I want to refer in this context to the interventions, mentioned above, of the Council fathers. The interventions which were the most impressive, and not only for us Protestants, were the same ones that were dictated by a deep biblical faith. I have shown in another place[4] how not only the so-called progressives but also the conservative Council fathers (Cardinal Ruffini, for example) constantly quoted the Bible; on the other hand, however, the manner of citation was highly questionable, especially in the first drafts. Texts which were taken out of context and which alluded only to certain words and not to the thought of the Schema were brought in as "proof texts." True, Cardinal Bea, by his interventions in which he found fault with this method, contributed to the elimination in most places in the final texts of exegetical caprice in this regard. This caprice is related to the fact that to many of the Council fathers, insofar as they were not biblical theologians, the biblical foundation as method was still unfamiliar.

A single arbitrary exegesis concerning the Virgin Mary has certainly remained in the final chapter of "De Ecclesia." It is a question of the methodology by which the text has explained the important passage, Mark 3:21-25. Because Mary fulfilled the will of God, she is arbitrarily figured in with those of whom Jesus spoke when He said that those who fulfill the will of God are His mother, brothers, and sisters. However, the passage clearly means to *contrast* true relatives with the blood relatives—Mary, brothers, and sisters—who are outside asking for Him. The context of the Scripture passage directly opposes the interpretation in the chapter.

For all that, in no council has the endeavor to ground collected statements in the Bible endured in the same way.

In the following I wish, without going into details, to show how—apart from the manner of quoting—on decisive points in the Council texts the Bible directly inspired the new reform

[4] See the article, "The Bible in the Council," *Dialogue on the Way*, edited by G. Lindbeck (Minneapolis, 1965), pp. 129-144.

thinking which is contained in the different constitutions and decrees. In this respect the Bible was not only consulted after the texts had been written but gave impetus to important statements from the beginning.

I have already mentioned that the ecumenical character which John XXIII wished to see realized flowed essentially out of the biblical principle of renewal. It is also symptomatic that the greatest biblical theologian of the Council, Cardinal Bea, has become the first president of the newly created Secretariat for the Christian Unity.

Thus we are not surprised that the text concerning ecumenicity, worked out by Cardinal Bea, breathes the spirit of the Bible. In fact, new value for non-Catholic Christians and non-Catholic churches has come about in Catholicism directly out of the biblical methodology which is rooted in salvation history. The static concept of heresy has disappeared. In this decree the new recognition, inspired by salvation history, that God and the Holy Spirit have been and are still at work in the non-Catholic churches has stepped into its place. Not only a new-style concept of ecumenism but also a new-style concept of the Church is visible here: the Roman Church is not the exclusive one which absorbs all others, and the others are no longer mere objects of conversion. The relationship to us is no longer sought in view of our "return." Our individualities are even evaluated as special gifts of the Spirit. Everywhere direct or indirect reference is made to the history of salvation which comes out of the Bible.

If then, however, some sentences are called to mind that state that only the Catholic Church has the truth in its fullness, this simply confirms the statements made above concerning the limits of Catholic renewal: Catholicism cannot give up its fundamental dogmas. The problem is that the Catholic Church, without giving up its claim (which is, of course, unacceptable to us) to be the only true Church, nevertheless recognizes that our churches are also *Christian churches* and that Chirst has given us special gifts.

In the Constitution concerning the Church in a provisionally printed text a chapter concerning the hierarchy originally followed a chapter concerning the mystery of the Church. Perhaps under the influence of the discussions between non-Catholic observers and Council fathers, but certainly under the influence of several interventions of the bishops in the Basilica, an important chapter on the Church as "the wandering [pilgrim] people of God" has now been inserted between these. In this chapter the Church appears thoroughly biblical as the chapter describes the continuity of its God-led paths (including the deviations or detours) through history. Thus its eschatological alignment and its present temporality find consideration.

Thoroughly biblically oriented is the Constitution "De Sacra Liturgia" which was discussed and accepted in the first session. It stresses that God is present in Word *and* in sacrament. The entire text is carried by the spirit of the biblical salvation history. The worship service is placed in this framework as a representation of the great saving acts of God and also as a proleptic realization of that which we expect from the future on the basis of revelation. It is not astonishing that all practical consequences which result from this bring the Catholic worship service nearer the Protestant service. Now the congregation is taking part in an entirely different way: the vernacular has been brought into the service, the lay chalice guaranteed on certain occasions, communal singing recommended, and expository preaching encouraged. Naturally it may not be overlooked, here as everywhere, that it is a Catholic text, and the worship service remains Catholic.

Furthermore the text concerning the laity goes back to the Bible. Again it must be said that we as Protestants would have to say something more, but this should not cause us to overlook the fact that within the limits of the existing dogmas concerning the Catholic hierarchy, seldom-heard biblical notes have been sounded concerning the charisma of the laity in the Church. Moreover, these find practical application in the creation of a ministerial council appointed by the bishop in which the laity should be strongly represented. We see that in every place where the Bible is the foundation, a correct deeper ecumenical attitude is also present. Thus we read in this text the wonderful sentence,

"Through working together with other churches the Catholic laity renders an account as a witness for Christ, Saviour of the World, and for the unity of the human family."

The Decree concerning missions shows, again in connection with the Bible, how mission as a task of the end times has its place in the present in the plan of God in salvation history. It is especially pleasing that working together with the missions of the non-Catholics has been recommended here.

A text deserves special mention in this regard, a text to which the outsider has not so far done sufficient justice among the different Council documents: the one concerning "Education for the Priesthood." In my opinion it belongs to the best and most important of the texts. Here the study of the Bible is placed as the foundation of dogmatics, while the Thomistic elements which were predominate previously move entirely into the background. This text, moreover, is suited more than all the others to influence the effects of the Council in the future. If the future education of the priests is carried out in accordance with this principle, the progress of the Catholic Church in the direction of the biblical thinking in terms of salvation history is secured.

Many particulars might be mentioned in this regard about the text concerning the "Community Orders," in which the return to the Gospel is placed before the return to the rules of the order.

The "Declaration concerning the Jews" which was worked out by the Secretariat for Unity and which has stirred up so much dust has been made possible only because of the biblical principle of renewal. Israel is not looked at simply as a religion among others. On the contrary, in direct connection with the Bible a close relationship with the Church of Christ is stressed here. The death of Jesus may not be blamed on the people of Israel as a collective responsibility for all times. More than that the text recognizes Israel's permanent role in the events of salvation (Heilsgeschehen) which concern the Church in the present and future. In the Pauline sense it is brought out that God remains true to His covenant with this people, continues to grant to Israel His special gift of grace, and calls it to its destiny.[5]

---

[5] See Augustine Cardinal Bea, "Das jüdische Volk und der göttliche Heilsplan," Stimmen der Zeit (1965), pp. 641ff.

The striking out of two words in the final text which had stood in the provisional draft is certainly regrettable but should not be exaggerated, as it has been in the papers, in view of the gratifying fact that the text has been drawn up. The words are, on the one hand, "damned" *(condemnat)* which had stood in the passage in the original outline, according to which the Catholic Church condemned anti-Semitism. According to the present text, the Church only "disapproves" *(reprobat)* it. Decisive for the removal of the word "damned" was the consideration of the protests of the opponents from the East who were chiefly influenced by politics. They argued that the persecutor of other minorities would not be covered with a judgment of condemnation by the Council, and that such condemnation should be shunned according to the opening speech of John XXIII.

This objection was certainly an excuse, a pretext, but nevertheless the dispute over the word should not have been blown out of proportion by those on the other side. In spite of this concession the text itself still speaks out in all clarity against anti-Semitism. Indeed no one would have taken the slightest offense to the simple "disapproves" if "damned" had not stood in the earlier outline.

Stronger yet, on the other hand, and with a passion even less suitable to the importance of the thing, is the argument for and against the retention of the word *deicida,* which was likewise contained in an earlier outline. The present text explains in an explicit manner that neither the entire people of Israel at the time of Jesus, nor even less the Jewish people of today, are guilty of the execution of Jesus. However, the original draft contained besides that the sentence which says that the Jewish people may not be accused of the "murder of God." This sentence has been struck out in the final draft, and again as a concession to the Eastern bishops and also to the non-Roman orthodox ecclesiastical people and theologians who showed themselves to be at least as vehement opponents of the Jewish declaration as the Catholic bishops of the East. It is not worthwhile to go into the elaborate arguments of the opponents[6] which would only show that these

6 See Gregory Baum, "The Conciliar Statement on the Jews," *The Ecumenist* (1966), pp. 27ff.

arguments masked the true reason for their opposition: their political hostility toward the Jews. Nevertheless, the basis of the concession by the Secretariat for Unity is weak. But, as it has been pointed out, the entire thing is only a dispute about a word. Even without this word the rejection of the collective guilt of the Jewish people in the death of Jesus has been expressed with all clarity in the final text.

Something other appears to me much more regrettable from the biblical standpoint regarding the Declaration about the Jews: in connection with the politically inspired protests of the Arabian states against this Declaration, which they wished to suppress entirely, this Declaration has not been accepted as an ingredient in the Constitution concerning the Church, where it belonged. Neither did it figure as an independent Declaration, which would not have been too bad. But it has been aligned in the Declaration concerning *non-Christian religions*. To be sure this Declaration on non-Christian religions is in itself satisfactory, even though it might be better grounded in biblical thought. But in any case, the Declaration on the Jews does not belong in it. Israel now appears as a religion among the other non-Christian religions, if not according to the content of the Declaration at least by its alignment. This is not correct, however. Israel's relation to the Christian Church is something entirely different from its relation to other religions. Israel is the common root for Judaism and Christianity. In this false alignment lies a relapse into the unhistorical methodology of former Catholic theology. It is an absurdity for Islam to be spoken of before Israel. But this alignment was a diplomatic concession which was made chiefly in order to put through the satisfactory text in spite of political intrigues. When we consider how much the Ecumenical Council in Geneva allowed diplomatic caution to govern in this regard, we should recognize behind the blemish of the false alignment the courage of this Declaration. It also represents an important element in the renewal of the Catholic Church by purification and development in the return to biblical thinking.

Finally we have to speak once more about the fundamental

Constitution concerning the "revelation." We have already attempted in the foregoing paragraphs to point out especially in it the clear limit which is set to the reform on account of the necessity of respecting dogma. The same Constitution also allows us to put to test an example for the contention that return to the Bible is really the reforming principle of this Council. True, we have already seen that those unavoidable limits do not allow us to accept the Council statements about the relation of Scripture and tradition. However, on the other hand, we see now how the new role which Scripture is assigned must basically burst open the definition of that relationship and must place the Bible in a higher position in the sense of a standard, of a "norm."[7]

We can entirely agree with the exegetical principles which are stated in this Constitution. The human origin of Scripture, which is explained by the incarnation of Christ, is recognized. *Formgeschichte* and the distinction of literary families in the Bible are portrayed. The inerrancy of the Bible in the sense of verbal inspiration is abandoned, to be maintained only where it is a question of the truths which God, as it says, wants to point out for the sake of our salvation (*veritas, quam Deus nostrae salutis causa litteri sacris consignari voluit*). This formula can be traced to the interventions of Cardinal Koenig of Vienna who pointed out a series of discrepancies in the Bible. What we exegetes have seen in meetings of Old and New Testament associations for a long time is confirmed by these Council texts: the agreement between Catholic and Protestant exegetes is as good as achieved. It is not as if we would all agree in all exegetical questions. However, the borders of the different "schools" do not coincide any longer with the borders of the Catholic and Protestant confessions.

It should be mentioned also that joint labor with the separated brethren for the production of the *translation of the Bible* is expressly recommended in the official texts. And the study of Scripture is designated as "anima Sacrae Theologiae." It demands

[7] For a differently oriented discussion, see ". . . Concerning De Divina Revelatione," pp. 46-50.

that preaching, catechism, and all Christian instruction draw their healthy nourishment and their holy power out of Scripture.

Scripture, as this has already happened practically in the Constitution concerning the liturgy, is in principle equated by appeal to the Church fathers to the sacrament of the Eucharist, and the presence of God in Scripture is expressed as strongly as has ever occurred even from the Protestant side. We read here the impressive sentence, "God comes to His children in Scripture and holds dialogue with them." We could not say it better.

True, the joy over this passage was tarnished for the Protestant observers at the end of the third session. The Pope, right at the last because of the pressure from the conservative Council fathers, altered a similar sentence in the text on ecumenism which had expressed the same thing of the Bible reading of the Protestants. In the original text it had said, "stimulated by the Holy Spirit, the Protestants find *(invenuit)* God in the Holy Scriptures." Now it says, because the sentence has been given a subjective sense, "calling upon *(invocantes)* the Holy Spirit, the Protestants seek *(inquirunt)* God in the Scriptures as the One who speaks to them." Had this stood from the beginning, the manner of expression would have hardly caused offense. We recall Pascal's words, "You would not seek me if you had not found me." Only the alteration was offensive. The Protestant observers could determine the alteration from the earlier outline, which had been handed with complete confidence to them as to the Council fathers, as were all other printed Council outlines which were to be kept secret. The alteration was a concession to the conservative fathers. It might have prevented worse alterations to the text on ecumenism, alterations which they had demanded at the same time as this one. The concession was justified by the fact that according to other texts of the Council, Scripture can be completely understood only in relation to tradition and the teaching office of the Catholic Church, according to Catholic teaching, which remains valid even now. Thus, in the last analysis, even this much discussed alteration belongs in the previous chapter which dealt with the "limits" of Catholic reform.

An examination of the Council texts as well as the events of the Council permits us to conclude with certainty that Vatican Council II is actually a reform of the entire Catholic Church and teaching, a reform which comes from the Bible. The resulting higher valuation of the Bible which is universally recognized is not, as is customarily described, one element among others. It is the theological principle to which the others were subordinated, even the *aggiornamento* which is often considered the true principle of the reform by this Council.

Indeed to a certain extent, both in many texts and also in many of the things which took place at the Council, there has been modernization without this subordination to a predominant theological theme. But, we do not believe, according to all that has been said up till now, that the true significance of the Council is to be sought there. With this reservation, we must now turn to this aspect.

3. AGGIORNAMENTO

It is the task of all preaching and all theology to bring the gospel near to the modern world. When the gospel stepped into the world of the first century, the apostles were confronted with this duty to preach a gospel which was foreign to the men of that time—"scandal" and "foolishness" (1 Cor 1:23)—so that they understood it. Since the world changes in every century, and since, moreover, always and at any time new areas with different cultures are brought into Christianity as a consequence of the mission endeavor, the problem always appears anew. Thus every era must formulate the old confession and discuss theology with the contemporary world.

In former times Catholicism has adapted itself, most unconsciously, to the world of each era. On the one hand, it often went too far in this accommodation. On the other hand, it sought in official documents to ward off the dangers of modernization which show up in this undertaking. Thus the problem was considered in a purely negative way. It condemned as so-called modernists those who endeavored to solve the problem positively. The encyclical "Humani Generis," which was proclaimed by Pius XII, enters into the problem of modernization, but in a negative way only; it only cautions against the dangers. At Vatican Council II the question about the positive side should have been raised and solved theologically for the first time. (As a practical problem it emerged earlier in connection with the mission methods of the Jesuits.) To that extent the *aggiornamento* stressed in this Council is a significant attempt for the history of the Church; nevertheless, it is theologically fruitful only to the extent that it is bound up simultaneously with the theological principle of the return to the Bible. Only then do prospects exist that the gospel really will be preached to the world.

We must distinguish precisely in *aggiornamento*—as has already been indicated—two tasks which are closely related to one another:

1. that of adaptation to the world of the external forms of the gospel, which remains unaltered in its kernel;

2. that of confrontation of the kernel of the gospel with the world and assimilation of such elements of the world which may be compatible with this kernel.

Vatican Council II was concerned with both tasks and has resolved them in many respects. If the fulfillment of the two tasks has not been accomplished all along the line, it is because the Council did consciously subordinate these tasks to the biblical principle of renewal, but rather made *aggiornamento* the superior concept and did connect this with a simultaneous return to the Bible. This is the consequence of the fact that the Council did not proclaim the biblical principle as the chief principle—although it practiced it in a satisfactory manner.

Both tasks of *aggiornamento,* adaptation of the form to the modern world and discussion with the world, require for their successful realization that at the same time the heart of the gospel be determined in its immutable essence.

To begin with, we will speak of the first task. It was formulated correctly by John XXIII in his opening speech on October 11, 1962: "The authentic teaching of the church should be studied and stated according to the methods of investigation and forms of expression which modern thinking uses. The substance of the old teaching which is contained in the deposit of faith is to be distinguished from the formulations in which it is dressed." Here a correct distinction between form of expression and substance has been made. Since the border between form and substance is fluid, perhaps distinction between variable elements and unalterable kernel would be preferable. Indeed John XXIII meant this also in reality.

Now, however, it must be pointed out that this distinction has only been formulated, not actually made, by the Council. Here the problem only begins, for now the task is to define what are forms of expression or variable elements and what is the unalterable substance or kernel. It seems to me that the Council, with regard to *aggiornamento*, suffered from the fact that this question was not clearly raised from the beginning, and that it was not even seen by many. For thus it happened that outsiders, and also a few Council fathers, did not escape the danger simply of finding everything which was modern good without questioning what, in that case, should now be modernized.

In no way do I maintain that the Council as such might have fallen into this danger but, rather, that it is responsible if in connection with this danger an extremism results from an enthusiastic fascination with everything modern. I think that the progressives should react strongly against this extremism just as the Reformers of the sixteenth century reacted against the extremists of that time. For otherwise they provide the conservative reaction against all reform with an all too comfortable area of assault.

In order to exclude any misunderstanding of the following remarks, I stress that I do not approve of the reaction of the conservative fathers against *aggiornamento,* which was rejected by them on principle. Their reaction had not been dictated by a concentration on the biblical center. The restrictions which were undertaken only out of diplomacy and not for the preservation of that center have nothing to do with the biblical and theological establishment of *aggiornamento.* It is regrettable that the reaction against an *aggiornamento* which lacked theological foundations came mostly from the circle of conservatives who were against any *aggiornamento,* instead of from those who earnestly sought a legitimate *aggiornamento.*

The question concerning the differentiation between unalterable center and variable elements proved to be the same for the Catholics as for the Protestants. However, the answer, namely a more detailed definition of the center, cannot be the same. I have indicated in the first part of this chapter that in Catholicism the dogmas belong to the center. We have seen how the Council has endeavored to respect the dogmas and yet at the same time how it has endeavored to allow a greater role to the Bible within the center than Catholicism up till now. The answer is much easier for Protestants, because we have to consider only the Bible in the definition of the kernel, while Catholics have to include the dogmas. However, if the problem of defining the unchangeable center had been consciously raised, the Catholic discussion concerning the relationship between Scripture and tradition in this special light—in connection with the higher valuation of the Bible—would have undergone a greater deepening, and would have brought us closer. The definition of the kernel is really our common problem even if it cannot be solved in the same way.

The fact that many times the necessity of making the distinction between center and variable elements was not seen as a problem to be consciously dealt with in the Council enterprise of *aggiornamento* could perhaps be connected with the fact that the Catholic Church does not have the same practical experience as Protestantism in the positive theological endeavor of clothing the gospel in modern forms of expression. However, the latter has not solved the problem either. We see today that a part of American Protestantism in its thoroughly legitimate endeavor to take into consideration the contemporary secular world obviously overlooks the distinction between center and forms of adaptation even more than the Council. It does not observe the limits which must be set in modernization. If similar tendencies in a more moderate form would not also be discernible in more recent times in European Protestant theology, tendencies which might even have given impetus to extreme positions in America, one would attempt to explain the present American radicalism and the extremely naïve and uncritical belief in progress from the fact that American Protestant theology in former times has not experienced in the same degree as the European the crisis of growth in the discussion with the "world." The powerful sensation that every publication stirs up in America at the present may, in any case, be connected with that. With an astonishing unconcern the Christian message in these works concerning "secularization," in which Bonhoeffer is appealed to hardly with justification, is given a new demythologizing interpretation, until no element of the message remains which would be a "scandal" or "foolishness" to the modern man. Generally it is not asked afterward if that which was the vital part of the message for the men of the Bible has been abandoned.

I have only mentioned these publications and slogans which have become sensations and which presently influence wide circles of Protestantism in America to show by an extreme example the consequences of an *aggiornamento* as they appear in the case of a disregard of center and variable elements. True, the apostle is a Jew to the Jews (1 Cor. 9:20) and a Greek to the Greeks, but, on the other hand, he allows the "scandal" and the "foolishness" to stand as such, because they belong to the essence of the gospel. He is not ashamed of it, neither before the "world" of the pagans nor before that of the Greeks, as he writes in Rom. 1:14ff. The book of Acts confirms this in connection with the story about Paul's sermon on the Areopagus, where the apostle agrees with the Athenians—as far as it is possible for him—but does not hesitate to speak of the resurrection of Christ, unconcerned that he thereby evokes the laughter of his hearers.

The gulf between the gospel and the secular world is stressed with reason today. It is false, however, to suppose that this gulf may be decisively greater today than the gulf which separated the world of that time from the gospel. Indeed there was no technocracy, and the present "secular city" is different from the ancient "polis." But with regard to the pretension that the salvation of mankind shall depend upon that which happened to a man, Jesus Christ, even at that time the Athenians had to laugh. The scandal already existed.[8]

Notice was not always taken at the Council that the more urgent the question concerning modernization is, the more earnest the effort for a deeper understanding of the kernel should be. Above all it had to be recognized that the heart of the gospel is scandal and foolishness for the understanding.

In some texts of the Council this character of scandal has been hidden in several places by the scholastic substructure of natural theology, therefore in the final analysis by the suppression of the biblical substance by philosophy. For that reason intellectual applications of *aggiornamento* in the Constitutions and Decrees do not satisfy. They place rational arguments ahead of biblical substance. It matters little if the adaptation to modern thought forms is too radical or not radical enough. Modernization of the forms of expression can be pushed *very far* if only that which John XXIII called the "substance" does not get lost because of it.

The history of Catholic theology has to exhibit a warning for Catholicism (as also, moreover, for Protestantism) precisely against permitting the necessary adaptation of the center to modern thought forms to be smothered by modern philosophies. Precisely this has been the fate of Catholic theology. It widely adapted in the Middle Ages to the bulk of the then modern Aristotelian speculative concepts and, therefore, lost the biblical foundation and biblical thought. Paradoxically, because of the retention of this unguarded medieval *aggiornamento,* it became separated from the world. We have seen that Vatican Council II precisely in every point where it accomplished real reforms, has replaced the static-scholastic concepts with biblical ones. In this way it has become *contemporary.* If the Church of today is made to stand in the living stream of that special history which connects it with the biblical source, the alignment of the present in these events remains of pressing importance, for the present time and for all times. In no case should the Church progress

---

[8] Important for these paragraphs is "The Theology of Salvation History . . .", esp. the last few pages.

further on the path of too much adaptation, even if it is a question of the ruling philosophies of the day.

The inquiry concerning the center has to be considered much more carefully in the second task which I have mentioned above and which is related to *aggiornamento*: the task of objectively confronting the gospel with the world, of understanding the world, of making clear its position, meeting it and assimilating the things which are compatible with the gospel, in order in this manner to facilitate the dialogue with it. Again it must be said that this program is not only legitimate but necessary. It must be our concern to make the gospel understandable to the world, being careful that it really is the gospel that we are explaining.

This task has now been begun by the Council, above all in the much discussed text about "The Church in the World of Today," indirectly also in the Declaration concerning "Freedom of Religion." These two texts were considered the most important by outsiders and the newspapers, by some as the only important documents. Indeed they are an especially clear example of the modernization of the Catholic Church, of the *aggiornamento*. In fact it is an important event that a Council has been concerned with this question. The fact in and for itself that the Church recognizes itself accountable in this manner for events in the world belongs as such on the line of the biblical ethic. In spite of this the more theological Council texts appear to me to be even more important for the further working of the desire of renewal, especially the ones which return to the Bible behind every kind of undergrowth that comes from an illegitimate accommodation. For from both tasks which belong to every reform, adaptation is less necessary than purification for the Catholic Church, because adaptation belongs to its essence anyway.

The attitude to the world as the designated texts try to define it is a courageous but difficult and dangerous undertaking. The danger seems to me to have been not altogether recognized by the authors of the documents. We are pleased about the brave and, in part, extremely valuable expositions of these texts, especially the one concerning religious freedom which has to alter the situation of the Protestants in certain predominantly Catholic countries. It must, nevertheless, be said about the Constitution concerning the Church in the world that it is not sufficiently grounded in the specifically Christian revelation, in spite of all good intentions. In many cases that is due to the design which, according to the traditional Catholic schema of the scholastics, places the rational arguments before the foundation of revelation.

In the Basilica of St. Peter the Council fathers repeatedly stated, and the observers stressed it in the discussions which were organized by the Secretariat for Unity, that we as Christians may not be satisfied by simply saying the same thing as the world— even if it is something impressive. We must say it differently and say different things wherever possible, even things which the world does not like to hear or has trouble understanding.

It would be unjust, as I have said, not to mention that the texts have been written with this concern in mind. And yet they are not completely satisfactory in this regard. The danger of eliminating the scandal which belongs to the gospel and of solving the problem "gospel and world" in an all too comfortable manner should have been reacted against more strongly. They have not always avoided the danger of eliminating everything which causes difficulties in the matching of the two factors, gospel and world, and of taking secular values from the world with no concern if they are compatible with the gospel or not. The Church should not forget its prophetic role toward the world in its effort to come into conversation with the world. On the other hand, it is true that we should beware of every pietistic opposition to the world and of every rejection of its values. However, we do not overcome this false pietistic attitude if we go to the opposite extreme and present everything secular as if willed by God and compatible with the gospel. I refer here again to the extreme position of certain modern Protestants for whom the modern world has plainly become the modern idol. Certainly the Council has not gone to this extreme, but the same danger emerges in the background in the Council texts in which the relation to the world is discussed. It is the ever-present danger as it has threatened Christianity intellectually and practically in the form of Gnosticism and then in medieval Catholicism: the danger of *syncretism.*

If there have been grievances in the Catholic Church in the past, it is because it has often proceeded on the way of syncretism, because it has secularized itself instead of subjecting the necessary entering into the world to the purifying principle of standardization to the Bible. The assimilation which Catholicism permits itself in the shaping of tradition in the earlier centuries is precisely that which makes it uncontemporary. That which is fortunately expressed in some Council texts, renewal by concentration on the biblical kernel and consequently the renewal by the elimination of the elements which cannot be assimilated, is not sufficently realized in the text concerning the world. The endeavor to look more for the positive in the secular values and to overstress the achievements of the world has led to the fact that the Constitution concerning "The Church in the World of Today" in many cases says things with a certain verbosity and diffuseness which the world also says—and in many cases perhaps better. It is true that outsiders are repelled at first by the "scandalous" character of the Christian message, but they nevertheless expect Christians to say more than that which can be read in every modern, also non-Christian and nontheologically trained, sociologist. Indeed we should assimilate that which might be assimilated, but then also only in order to move these elements into the new light of the gospel. However, that which cannot be assimilated should be designated as such without false shame.

The words of Paul in Rom. 12:2 have been rightly recalled at the Council: "Do not let the world squeeze you into its own mold, but be changed by the renewal of your understanding."

The dialogue with the world which began at Vatican Council II will go further, and we can already see how it is working out practically (e.g., the different papal trips). We can only hope that thereby the endeavor to permeate the world with the gospel might be stronger than that of altering the gospel by the world. The world should certainly be the object at which preaching and all the work of the Church should be directed. For that reason the

Church should know the world accurately. But the standard of all preaching and all the work of the Church should be the gospel and not the world. The danger of false connection with the world must be even more seriously regarded than it has at the Council. And to be sure, as already mentioned, this should happen from the side of the progressives, since the conservative reaction generally flows out of a false attitude which in principle opposes the dialogue with the world.

The danger of syncretism is that of false comprehensiveness, of false universality, which suppresses the true Christian universality. This occurs when reform is not understood simultaneously as concentration and purification.

Summing up everything said until now, we want, lastly, to attempt to answer in the light of church history the question whether the Council with its reforms represents only an undeviating continuation of the age-long endeavor of Catholicism to further extend its worldwide spiritual sphere of influence, or if it has, as every true reform should, conducted a self-critique and correction of earlier developments, or if and in which sense both have occurred.

4. CATHOLIC COMPREHENSIVENESS AND BIBLICAL CENTRALITY AT THE COUNCIL

The Catholic theologian Hans Küng writes an interesting assessment of the council, in which he determines a new attitude which is present in all areas:

"To explain this Council—as often happens today in Catholic theology—by the harmless concept of organic development (simply as a further extension of Catholic universality) may turn out to be an apologetic construction." According to Küng the Council was, rather, evidence of a reform in elimination of distortions: "Why may not a church, which according to universal Catholic opinion, can be mistaken also show that it is capable of a Christian conversion and correction?"

In opposition to this, but entirely independent of Küng's exposition, some Protestant theologians[9] indirectly agree in this respect with those Catholic theologians who are fought by Küng. Indeed they also look at the biblical renewal, such as the Conciliar extension of the dialogue, merely as quantitative broadening of the already present traditional Catholic comprehensiveness. They understand the reform of Vatican II only in the sense of an "addition," of a "development and supplement." For example, the Protestant observer W. Dietzfelbinger entirely agrees with them when he says, "Reform cannot be an appearance of something new and also not deliverance from something old which has proven to be false or obstructive for the church. Reform can only be development of something that was already present in embryonic form. What has been obstructive or false can be pushed back or perhaps even forgotten, but not cut out. What was once there disappears no more."[10]

Both assertions represent theological and ecclesiastical variants of the more popular conclusions mentioned above: "Nothing is changed," "everything is changed." Thereby it is interesting that the one represents the judgment of conservative Catholics and critical Protestants (certainly with different intentions) and the other the conclusion of a Catholic progressive.

Both contradictory judgments mention something which is correct. It is agreed that the catholicity of the Roman Catholic Church is capable of admitting from anywhere the most diverse elements in the framework of purely external unity: on the one hand, tradition with all of its unbiblical outgrowths (dogma of Mary!) and yet, on the other hand, also the Bible itself. It is further correct in a certain sense that this Council, in abandoning the anti-Protestant attitude, turns back behind the Counterreformation to medieval Catholicism and accepts, so to say, the Protestant and his interests (and first, quite correctly, the Ortho-

---

[9] For example, G. Maron in a stimulating article in *Materialdienst des konfessionskundlichen Instituts Bensheim*, entitled, "Der römische Katholizimus nach dem Konzil. Grundriss einer Analyse" (1966). This article belongs to the best of the articles published from the Protestant side since the close of the Council concerning the formulation of the question. The answer, as I wish to show, appears to me to be justified only in one respect.

[10] *Luth. Monatshefte* (1965), p. 578.

dox). It is further correct that, going consistently further along this path, the Council has endeavored to include in any kind of form the non-Christian religions and to come into a relationship with atheism. And it is correct that the pre-Reformation tendencies of Roman Catholicism have been further stimulated by the Council insofar as it has increased the rigidity of the external unity and, in connection with that, has resumed not only acceptance of worldly values but also the claim to be a decisive influence on the world (e.g., the speech of Pope Paul VI at the United Nations).

However, the undeniable fact exists, on the other hand, that, seen from the point of view of the Bible, Küng is also correct when he asserts that the Council means cleansing and purification. With these come correctives. Everything which we have outlined in the second section of this essay and have verified in the Council texts would be untenable if Vatican Council II meant only a return to pre-Reformation Catholicism and only organic development of the syncretistic tendencies which are contained therein.

Indeed, Catholicism has been quantitatively expanded, and we have seen in the previous sections that this expansion of the gospel is questionable in certain respects. But the consequent inclusion of the Bible in the combination of opposite elements which resulted at the Council has, as a result, that Catholicism has pushed an element of contraction and purification into the foreground along with that partially problematic expansion. This element of purification must effect the entire nature of Catholicism from inside out as a critical ferment of elimination of illegitimate elements.

True, we have seen that as usual the Bible theoretically has not been elevated to the standard which stands over the tradition and the teaching office. But wherever, in spite of this, a sincere effort is effectively present, as at the Council, to allow renewal from the Bible, there the indwelling power of its judicial function penetrates all theories which are oriented to something other and opposes them in exercise of its claim to be the exclusive standard. As soon as one really permits himself to be inspired from the Bible, it *cannot* be simply one element *among others* in the *complexio oppositorum* (mixture of opposites). It must lead to the cleansing of the entire *complexio*.

Thus more has happened at this Council than a reaching back behind the Counter-reformation to the Catholicism of the Middle Ages which Luther fought. Certainly the pre-Reformation Catholicism possessed the Bible. We know that even before the Reformation it had once and again broken through the hard stone of tradition in many places; otherwise the Reformation would not have been possible. But never has the Bible captured the position which this Council at least endeavored to concede to it.

Therefore, the Catholic Church in Vatican Council II not only goes back behind the Counter-reformation, but even behind the Middle Ages. It goes back to the Bible, and as a result there has been some elimination of illegitimate elements along with the occasionally questionable expansion of Catholic universality. Thus the situation is not exactly the same as at the time of Luther, who himself saw only that syncretistic Catholicism which he fought. The biblical centrality which Luther carried out has been at work at the Council—and certainly not without his indirect influence—though alongside the opposite stream of limitless climbing expansion.

Catholicism has become "complexio oppositorum" in a new sense at this Council: it does not exist any longer only as a co-existence of added opposite elements. It is now, rather, ruled by two opposing chief tendencies, from two movements—by the old movement toward all-embracing Catholic breadth and by the new movement toward concentration.

We must certainly stress over against the Catholic progressives —and to be sure in the interest of true ecumenism which, in distinction to fashionable ecumenism, does not conceal the remaining differences—that there are elements which we Protestants cannot accept but which have been expressly retained at the Council: Tradition (Mariology), primacy of the Pope, overstressing of worldly values. And yet we find now in the light of the two movements which are discussed here (Catholic universality, biblical concentration) our chief thesis confirmed concerning the unrelated coexistence of the two lines of statements toward a goal of minimizing the importance of the old dogmas. The historical significance of the Council exists in that within the framework of completely Catholic principles, a biblical purification has nevertheless simultaneously occurred and certainly without organic connection.

Someone raised the interesting question if the reason why Catholicism can afford today to go back behind the Counter-reformation is because Protestantism in fact already may have abandoned its specific character, may have abandoned the principles of the Reformation, and therefore no longer represents a danger to Catholicism. There may be an element of truth in that statement, but it is not the whole truth. I want to ask from my own viewpoint if this Council and a biblical renewal within the given limits would have been possible without the positive influence from the side of the Protestants. Since the Council has not removed the danger of syncretism, I think it will be even more essential for Catholicism to have alongside it a Protestantism which does not go still further than Catholicism in syncretistic secularization, but which in every necessary adaptation stresses biblical centrality in preaching to the world. Seen from this point of view, not fusion but a federation of the churches is desirable as the goal of ecumenism. Catholicism needs alongside it a Protestantism which does not place the biblical centrality alongside universalistic tendencies without any connection as Catholicism does, but which consciously makes the Bible a higher standard for preaching to the world.

In this regard the question should then be asked if it is not likewise wholesome for Protestantism to have Catholicism next to it. On the one hand, Protestantism might remain conscious of its constant duty to react against the danger of Catholic syncretism. On the other hand, it could learn from Catholicism the positive side of universality. It might learn not to become narrow in its pursuit of biblical centrality. The centrality of the gospel should lead to a true, biblical universality. The catholicity of the Roman Church not only places the danger of syncretism before us, but also the duty of the legitimate and true Christian universality. In this regard perhaps there have been biblical elements lost in Protestantism which are still present in Catholicism. In any case we should ask ourselves if a "too little" in Protestantism does not stand opposite a "too much" in Catholicism. Instead of a biblical centrality being placed without a real link next to the broadening tendency of Catholic tradition, as has happened many times at the Council, a biblical universality which is protected against all syncretism must grow out of that centrality. To that end Catholicism should remind Protestantism not to lose sight of the goal of Christian universality. And Protestantism should warn Catholicism against the danger of falling into syncretism.

V

The Role of the Observers
at the Vatican Council

A farewell address given to the Secretariat for Christian Unity by Professor Oscar Cullmann in the name of the observers.

AT THIS TIME, when we are making reservations on planes and trains in order to return to our countries on various continents, and when we are already giving thought to the work which awaits us in our churches and universities, we wish to thank you not only for the invitation which you once again have extended to us, but also for the manner in which you have offered your hospitality and for the special character which you have given to our function as observers. Indeed, it is as observers that you have invited us; and this evening I would like to say several words concerning this role of observer. Since this Council is not a council for union but rather one of internal Catholic renewal, I find that it is completely normal that we should not speak but, rather, listen in the official sessions, and that we do not need to express our feelings by applause or by vote. But in this framework you have treated us nonetheless as observers of a special kind, and for this reason we would especially thank you.

It is impossible to be an observer from a distance, to look and listen coldly and without interior participation in that which is happening. If you had considered us as observers of this type and treated us in that way, I am certain that our presence here instead of uniting us would have further separated us. I am not speaking diplomatically, but with a concern for the truth! May

I say that it is our heart itself which shapes our statements. When Christians invite other Christians as observers, this function must inevitably take on a new meaning which cannot be that of an observer at a distance. Several weeks ago, in his private library, Pope Paul VI told us that he wished to express by this audience the fact that your Church wishes to permit us to observe not only from the doorway but from the interior of the house.

Because of the kindness of Your Eminence, Msgr. Willebrands, Msgr. Arrighi, Msgr. Duprey, and all your colleagues, we have lived all these weeks—far from our customary obligations—not next to you but with you in faith and in a friendly and cordial atmosphere. Administratively there is perhaps a difference between "delegates of the Church" and "guests." But, in fact, we are all treated like guests and not like distant observers. You have permitted us to share your preoccupations, your concerns, your emotions, your joys. You have even been interested in our leisure and have offered us opportunities for delightful excursions.

Because of your kindness, for two months we have formed a sort of community among ourselves in close connection with you. This community has become visible every morning in our gallery in St. Peter's. I said in a press conference that the historians of the Council ought to speak of the ecumenical role of the "bars," but it will be especially necessary to speak of the ecumenical role of this gallery, and in writing the history of the Basilica of St. Peter, it will be necessary to mention one day the ecumenical importance of this platform situated below the statue of Longinus.

Just as we have not been distant observers, neither is this gallery itself a distant observatory. It is located in the heart of the *aula,* and this is symbolic. It testifies to what is already possible from the ecumenical point of view: bringing together observers from non-Catholic churches, separated themselves by profound divergences and yet united at the World Council of Churches. But in a special way we have been fraternally united with the members of your Secretariat in this gallery under the paternal gaze—Your Eminence will permit me to employ this expression—of Cardinal Bea, whom we saw with joy opposite us at the top of the tier of the cardinals.

Your Secretariat is remarkable in that, although being an internal organ of the Vatican, by definition it is found in a close relation with non-Catholics. If this were only a diplomatic relationship it would not achieve its end, but you have truly succeeded in giving it this personal character which is so important from the ecumenical point of view. Because of the personal relations which you have succeeded in creating, your Secretariat is the open door of the Catholic Church toward the non-Catholic churches.

I have said that this Council is not a council for union. But the manner in which you have permitted us to be observers at a Catholic Council, to see what happens among you when you discuss your own internal questions, unites us perhaps even more than a Council for unity because it establishes an atmosphere of confidence so essential for the ecumenical dialogue. Rightly or wrongly, we have often reproached the Catholic Church in the past for what happens internally. Nevertheless, in everything which concerns this Council, you have hidden absolutely nothing. There is no "iron curtain" here. You have permitted us to observe not only the triumphal face of your Church, which we have been accustomed to seeing, but also the difficulties with which you have found yourself engaged. We can assure you that it is precisely through these difficulties that salvation history advances, all the more because they are related to the breath of renewal which we feel vitalizing your Church. Precisely in giving us an account of your difficulties, we realize that we find ourselves with you, in spite of those things which separate us, on the same road, in the same period of salvation history—an intermediary period of history in which there is almost certainly a proleptic realization of the Kingdom which is to come, but a period which is not the End and in which, consequently, the difficulties remain.

That is why we thank you for permitting us to observe openly all that happened, and for encouraging us to express our criticisms quite frankly and without reserve in our Tuesday meetings with Msgr. Willebrands, and to state these criticisms expressly from the point of view of our churches. If a proof is still necessary that you do not consider us distant observers, these Tuesday meetings furnish it in signal fashion.

On our side we are able to respond to these possibilities which you offer us only by making an effort to be other than aloof observers, to fully live this Council with you. To be sure, we ought not to suppress our critical spirit, but we should criticize with a desire to understand. The problem of the Church which has been discussed by the Council is also a problem for us. We pose it differently, as we have said quite frankly to you. But we also feel that the efforts to restore importance to the collegiality of the bishops and to the laity help to unite us.

You can imagine our inward emotional response to the Schema on ecumenism and the related discussions. In spite of everything which we have been able to say to you concerning certain aspects of this Schema, we all consider it as an ecumenical event, since for the first time an official text emphasizes what positive elements exist even in that which separates us and which traces this separation back to the diversity of the gifts of the Spirit. We thank all those who have collaborated on it.

Your Conciliar work continues after the session, and we know that it will be particularly intense. Our role as observers will certainly be less important between the sessions, but up to a certain point it should also continue, though in different ways. Our relations with the Secretariat will not be entirely interrupted. On the other hand, I consider it a great problem, to which we have not given sufficient attention, that ecumenism, for the moment, is too much an affair among theologians. We ought to do our best to instruct the lay members of our churches to take note of other confessions, as your Secretariat has permitted us to do.

"Secretariat"—signifying administration and red tape—is, on the whole, a very prosaic name for an institution like yours. While it is an *institution,* it is both a *creation* of the Holy Spirit—since it is He who urges Christians toward unity—and an institution which till now has been *inspired* in its work by the Holy Spirit. Because of this, we have been able to be observers in the sense which I have tried to define this evening. In any case, until now you have escaped the danger of institutionalism to which our institutions too often succumb. You have not "quenched the Spirit."

I would like our individual churches, Eastern and Protestant, our different denominations, to have institutions of this kind, whether it be called the Secretariat for Unity or given some other name. (Although it is very important, it is not enough to have an Ecumenical Council.) These institutions would represent hands extended in the Holy Spirit, the one toward the other, and the Holy Spirit could only unite us. In regard to this twenty-first Council you know that I like to call to mind the first Council, that of the apostles of which the New Testament speaks. I would hope that we were inspired by this first Council. When St. Paul speaks of it, he mentions the hand of fellowship (Gal. 2). The apostles, divided by serious problems, to the end gave one another the hand of fellowship. We are separated but remain united by the *koinonia* in all its forms. When we return in several days, unity, to be sure, will not be achieved. But I am certain that this Council, thanks to the particular character which you have given to our role as observers, will have created from now on a *koinonia* which will bear its fruits for our churches.

VI

Ecumenical Encounters at the Edge of the Council

Translated by Robert Holland from L. Kaufmann, Begegnung im Heiligen Land, *pages 167–168, Editor, Verlag C. J. Bucher A. G., Luzern, Switzerland.*

THE PRESENT COUNCIL has already been considered in different studies from the theological, liturgical, and pastoral points of view. Here we would like to speak of one aspect which at first glance seems to affect only the outward picture. However, in reality, for future relations between the Catholic Church and the other Christian churches, this aspect might have as important consequences as the texts achieved through the Council; by this I mean the personal contacts between the Council participants. These contacts have these characteristics: through several weeks the participants relinquished their own customs, forgot their own activities, all led the same life, followed the same "schedule," focused their interest on the same problems and to a large extent the same cares, shared the same joys and the same hopes. Nothing was so impressive as to follow the conversations—in spite of all the linquistic difficulties—of European, American, African and Asiatic, "Latin" and oriental Bishops.

Here, however, I would like to speak mainly of the contacts of the non-Catholic observers among themselves as well as of their contacts with the Council fathers. This Council had, for the observer, the surprising result that the personal bonds became closer among the Protestant and the Orthodox, who are bound together through the Ecumenical Council of Geneva, but this was not for the sake of a common opposition against those who had invited us. Many of us never before had the opportunity to live side by side with representatives of the various Orthodox churches, especially not with representatives of those churches with whom we have only recently been placed in a standing relationship, for instance, with those subject to the Patriarch in Moscow.

The daily encounters of the Protestant and the Orthodox groups permitted us to accumulate complex experiences which in their variety reflect well the present ecumenical situation. Often we noticed in our personal conversations as well as in our semi-public discussions, which were organzed each week for the observers and the Catholic theologians and Council Fathers, that in certain questions, the Orthodox and Catholic were united, in contrast to the Protestant, while in other questions, the Orthodox and Protestant were one and differentiated themselves from the Roman Catholics; that finally, in other questions, Protestant and Catholic agreed while the Orthodox stood alone. The latter situation was not infrequent and may be explained by a common Western heritage. This "crossing over" the border, which is important from the ecumenical point of view, was even more manifest because of the presence of representatives of the oriental churches who are united with Rome. The celebration of the Mass before the sessions,which periodically was held in various oriental rites and showed the same form as the Mass of the corresponding Orthodox Churches, indicated from the liturgical point of view the same complex situation which we noticed in the course of our theological contacts. All the same, in spite of the differences even among the observers which became visible through the colorful variations in their habits, we were reminded, speaking symbolically, by the platform which was reserved for us below the statue of Longinus, that all these Christians are united in the Ecumenical Council of Geneva, whereas here, they could only be observers of the Council. This double fact, which places in perspective the problem of unity, indicates at the same time the ecumenical possibilities and difficulties.

Yet, in spite of all this, there was no barrier between the

platform of the delegates and guests and the rest of the Basilica of St. Peter's. On the contrary, this seating arrangement will always keep its special historical meaning for the ecumenical movement. During this Council, it played an important role as the place of personal meeting. We were mixed there with members of the Vatican Secretariat for Unity and were together there with the Catholic translators. Even those among us who did not need a translation from the Latin were pleased to have specially competent interpreters beside them with whom they could often share their views as they were brought forth in the discussions. We had the impression that on this platform the ecumenical problem was practically solved and that there one forgot who were the Protestant and Orthodox observers and who were the Catholic. Then, there were the many visits on our platform: bishops and experts from the whole world had taken the custom of shaking our hands in greeting before the morning sessions, and at the end our Catholic friends waited for us below the platform. The main places of meeting were, however, the two refreshment stands in the side aisles of St. Peter's which carried the nickname "bar." Using a play on words, the German-speaking bishops called these places the "Lateral Council" (a variant of Lateran Council). If one were to write the history of this Council, he should speak of the role of both "bars," for without them the many bishops would certainly have found no opportunity to speak together. One had to see the overcrowded places where each one was standing with a cup of coffee in hand, commenting on the running discussions. It would have been very interesting to preserve certain of these conversations. These "bars" must be mentioned especially in an ecumenical regard. Our position as observer was easily recognized by our dress in the multitude of Catholic dignitaries, and we were surrounded by many; one asked for our opinion and we were happy to notice agreement so often. People learned to know each other in the most natural ways. Because of these "bars," I had the opportunity to meet famous Catholic theologians who previously were known to me only through their works; now they have become real persons to me. When I read their books, I see them again in the memory of these sympathetic surroundings. In these "bars" one often made other appointments besides the sessions, for meals together which one took by preference in one of the popular *ristorante* in the area of St. Peter's. The theological conversation at the same table—among brothers, whom one certainly can no more call "separated"—covered not only the newest anecdotes from the Council but often concerned the most serious questions. It also happened that bishops took us along in the car after the sessions so that we could eat with them in the various institutes where they had their common meal. Also we were often invited along with the Orthodox observers and once I ate at the same table with the famous, lively Patriarch of the Melkite Church, Maximus IV. I am convinced that all these contacts at the edges of the official sessions will bear for the Council fruits which we did not at first glance expect. Such personal contacts were indispensable for a successful theological discussion.

VII

The Ecumenical Task of Protestantism
after the Council

As PROTESTANTS, what can we learn from the Council? First and foremost that we should be ready at any time to renew ourselves also. It is not enough to say with pharisaic piety, "Praise God, at last the Catholics have become a little bit better!"; as if we ourselves had reached perfection! As if we might be able to say under the pretext that we have had our Reformation in the sixteenth century that we are renewed for all times. Certainly our renewal must appear different from the Catholic. It must consciously proceed from our foundation, the Bible. However, our churches are also in need of a renewal in the sense of a deepening. Every individual church—whether it be Lutheran, Reformed, Baptist, or whatever—should recollect its special gift (Charisma) and free itself from every malformation. Ecumenism dare not advance through the renunciation of individual gifts, but on the contrary, it must advance through an intensified faithfulness to purified individual gifts. Since every special gift has its roots in the *one* Gospel, correct unity in diversity will come in this manner.

In the final analysis renewal means conversion, repentance. Behind every true renewal which is more than a tendency toward anything that is new or modern, therefore behind every renewal which, as I have tried to point out, proceeds from a motif of faith, stands preparedness for conversion, repentance. This spirit of repentance which must force us, as the other (Catholics), to constant renewal will create correct ecumenical solidarity. For that reason we understand nothing of the renewal of the other if we ourselves do not renew ourselves.

Conversely, however, we will also not renew ourselves through the spirit of repentance, which is nothing other than the Holy Spirit, if we refuse to see the work of this Spirit in the other. Certainly we must recognize the borders which are set to every *Catholic* reform, and we must endeavor to point them out. But inside these borders we should recognize the work of the Holy Spirit. It is by no means a sign of individual renewal through the Holy Spirit if we wish to see in the other only evil spirits. On the contrary, it is instead a certain sign that we ourselves do not have this Spirit if we are not able to see that He works and where He works in the other.

The words of Paul in I Thess. 5:19 ff., "Test everything and hold fast to the best," will be cited again and again. But we should direct our whole attention above all to the fact that here Paul does not proceed from the negative but from the positive. We should notice that he does not use the Greek word "krinein" but a verb with a positive implication, "dokimazein." He does not say, "Criticize everything." He does not say, "Look only for that in others which you can attack." The first question should not be, "What is the other doing which is false?", but "What positive thing can I learn from them?" That should be our attitude to the Second Vatican Council.

But certainly we may and must also see, precisely from this attitude, the negative in the other and not pass over it in silence. Under the condition that we are ready to learn of the positive gifts of the other, we should also learn from the distortions, from the mistakes of the other, and strive in love to show these mistakes to the other, avoiding above all falling into them ourselves.

Thus, to be sure, a correct universality, as it has always been the goal of Catholicism, is one gift about which we should learn. But we must also see how this legitimate universality in Catholicism, even at the Council, always threatens to lose the foundation of the Gospel in an illegitimate breadth and to fall into syncretism, where the main concern is to enclose in a purely external unity all possible elements, untroubled thereby if these elements are compatible or not.

In all openness we should consider as our ecumenical task the labeling of this danger as such in the future. We should point out in Catholicism the places where it—seen in the light of the Gospel—already has fallen prey to this danger and where it might succumb to it in the future.

Unfortunately, there has arisen in connection with this Council a "fashionable ecumenism" which in part is stamped with a sentimental character. Today "ecumenism" has become a slogan, and this is not good for the thing itself. Not so very long ago it had taken courage to engage in ecumenical conversations and especially to work out ecumenical acts not only with the Orthodox but also with the Catholics. Today, conversely, opportunists can see in ecumenism a means by which to become famous, and now it takes courage to warn against ecumenical illusions.

All too often one can experience ecumenical conversations in which the Catholic partner stresses only how close Catholic teaching is now to Protestant. On the other hand, there are conversations where Protestant theologians, precisely to progressive Catholic theologians, give rise to the false impression that complete unity would be reached if the progressive party in Catholicism would ultimately be victorious. Certainly we should be happy about the things we have in common, and we should learn from each other. But we should not pass over in silence the divergencies which remain difficult even with the progressive. It is precisely these divergences about which we speak with one another. Even if we cannot eliminate them, it is progress nevertheless if we come to a better mutual *understanding* of them. It is, however, thereby necessary that the dialogue be carried on in full clarity and truth, not in confusion. If *then* an approximation of positions comes about, this is ultimately much more valuable. The danger exists today that those Protestants and Catholics who go as far as possible in ignoring or eliminating essential differences are designated as "ecumenically enlightened." This error should vanish. And certainly I do not want thereby to recommend as good ecumenists—this is the other contention—some of those who with the same one-sidedness on the opposite side systematically see only those things which separate us, and who now brush aside the Council by explaining that nothing has changed because of the Council.

We should not only designate as such the wrong ways which we see in Catholicism from a positive test in the light of the Gospel, but also above all we should learn from them. We have seen that we have the task of making the Gospel accessible to the modern era, a task which we have in common with the Catholics. Precisely in this connection, however, we should be careful to avoid on our side certain errors into which Catholicism in view of its past has fallen and even in the present still falls. Truly our permanent task must also be going out into the world. The question, "How do we preach in today's world?" cannot be lost to us. We must make ourselves understood to the world, adapt ourselves, but we should not thereby betray the Gospel. We should remain mindful of Paul's words which refer to the kernel of our message (Rom. 12:2), "Do not be conformed to this world, but be transformed by the renewal of your mind. . . ." The question concerning the unchangeable kernel and the variable outer forms must be asked by us in all sharpness precisely when we strive to make the Gospel understandable to the world. We should not preach to the world anything which it already knows and knows even better than we, but quite certainly the Gospel of which we should not be ashamed (Rom. 1:16) even in confrontation with the philosophers. We should also ask ourselves if the scandal over which the Athenians laughed does not belong for time eternal to the Gospel.

In the past Catholicism has adapted itself *all too much* to the world both in ecclesiastical life (taking over of pagan superstitions) and especially in theology (Scholasticism), without asking the question concerning compatibility with the kernel. And we must ask ourselves if the danger of expanding the "complexio oppositorum" in a way that the Christian foundation drops out of sight and an unbounded syncretism results is not still present.

We have seen that the greatest and abiding achievement of this Council has been that, with the intense higher valuation of the Bible, an element of purification has been pushed into the foreground, the established element which must lead to an elimination of all unassimilatable ingredients, an element which must check and rebuke syncretism within the proper borders.

It should be the task of Protestantism to help Catholicism on the path of purification, to advance the battle against all syncretistic tendencies. Protestantism means concentration on the kernel of the Gospel and from there elimination of all elements foreign to that kernel. Protestantism will cease to fulfill its mission over against Catholicism if it does not remain conscious of this, its innermost essence. It will lose its right to exist if it, under the slogan "secularization" and under the motto "world come of age" which bears the imprint of Bonhoeffer but which is widely falsely understood, pushes forward on its side an unbounded and unrestrained adaptation to the world and encourages syncretism. We give thereby a very poor example to Catholicism if we, instead of preaching the Gospel to the world of today, divest the Gospel of its indwelling character of scandal and raise the modern world as the norm. It is not necessary that we say to the modern world that which it already knows and says even better than we. This results in a false secularization of the Gospel which leads to a syncretism in which the Gospel becomes extinct. (Catholicism has never entirely surmounted this danger, which had been a danger to the life of Christianity in the Gnosticism of the second century, even if it is now more strongly protected against it by the higher valuation of the Bible at the Council.) Catholicism needs Protestantism alongside of it, but a Protestantism which is aware of its task of keeping syncretism at a distance, Nevertheless, if we ourselves walk on the path of syncretism and go even farther along it, we not only perform a great disservice to our Catholic brothers, but we also become the gravediggers of Protestantism. For Catholic syncretism protects against the complete destruction of the Gospel to some extent through the outer unity of the Catholic Church. To be sure, the form of this unity also seems to us to be secularization, and sooner or later the Gospel will suffocate here also.

Next to the already mentioned sentimental ecumenism the worst degeneration which threatens us today after the Council is an ecumenism which strives for unity in a *mutual surrender of the substance of Christianity.* Unfortunately, we determine all too often today that syncretistic secularization of the Gospel goes hand in hand with the disintegration of the evangelical kernel.

Correct ecumenism goes on a contrasting path. Correct ecumenism means finding, instead of the distortions which lead to separation, the original gift of each church in its essence which is anchored in the Bible. For what the original gift was, source of riches of the Gospel and mutual enrichment, was many times distorted in the passing of the centuries and has become an element of separation. For although all gifts (gifts of the Spirit) are different from one another, they are nevertheless, in so far as they are purified, manifestations of the same Spirit and must thereby bring us together. Therefore, our goal is not fusion but federation. The Spirit does not want unity in political coordination but unity in the diversity of gifts. Not in that we mutually capitulate before the modern world in a mutual renunciation of the Christian gifts, but in that we allow mutual renewal through the Holy Spirit in each of our churches, we perform a service both to ourselves and to the world for which the church of Christ is summoned.